HELP!
THERE'S A GUEST AT MY TABLE!

ANNABEL FRERE

Photography by Myburgh du Plessis

From the author

If you like a book with a happy ending, this one has many! Following on from *Help! There's a Stove in My Kitchen*, which introduces you to the basics of cooking, it's time to move on, into the world of the young professional, with encouragement to try your own variations and make a recipe your own. This book is designed to add to your repertoire of fun and effortless recipes, as well as give tips and suggestions for easy entertaining, from informal gatherings to well-organised occasions. And you'll find plenty of ideas for 'dressing up' dishes to add a little finesse for that extra appeal.

The secret to happy entertaining is to be well prepared, so that you can enjoy the company of your friends without being tied to the kitchen. To make it easy, there are tips on preparing foods in advance, and I've included guidelines on how long a recipe will take to make. I've also provided information on combining dishes to achieve balance in a meal, so that friends don't go home clutching bloated stomachs, and there are some table décor ideas, to make an occasion a bit special.

Thank you to the wonderful publishing team who not only took on this book, but welcomed me into the Penguin Random House South Africa family and did such a magnificent job of designing both *Help! There's a Stove in my Kitchen* as well as *Help! There's a Guest at My Table*.

Thanks also go to my family and friends, who are ever supportive of my culinary experiments. Martin, Georgie and Vicky have been especially helpful, and after a few months of tastings, a home roast is promised! Our latest family buzz word is 'artisan', which captures the style and care taken in creating the recipes in this book. Enjoy!

Annabel Frere

Published in 2018 by Struik Lifestyle, an imprint of Penguin Random House South Africa (Pty) Ltd
Company Reg. No. 1953/000441/07
The Estuaries, 4 Oxbow Crescent, Century Avenue, Century City 7441, Cape Town, South Africa
PO Box 1144, Cape Town, 8000, South Africa
www.penguinrandomhouse.co.za

PUBLISHER: Linda de Villiers
DESIGN MANAGER: Beverley Dodd
EDITOR: Cecilia Barfield
PROOFREADER AND INDEXER: Joy Clack
PHOTOGRAPHER: Myburgh du Plessis
STYLIST: Lisa Clark
STYLIST'S ASSISTANTS: Amber Ryan, Alex Levett, Kimberly Wood

Reproduction: Resolution Colour (Pty) Ltd
Printing and binding: 1010 Printing International Ltd., China

ISBN 978-143230-872-8

FSC
www.fsc.org
MIX
Paper from responsible sources
FSC® C016973

Penguin Random House is committed to a sustainable future for our business, our readers and our planet. This book is made from Forest Stewardship Council® certified paper.

CONTENTS

Bread Plate

Bread Knife

Dessert Spoon

Dinner Fork

Fish Fork

Salad Fork

GETTING ORGANISED

Serviette

Water Glass

Red Wine Glass

White Wine Glass

Cake Fork

Dinner Plate

Dinner knife

Salad knife

Soup Spoon

Fish knife

First decide on the kind of gathering you want; will it be drinks and snacks with finger foods, where everyone can mingle and walk around with a plate in hand, or a buffet-style meal where you help yourself from a few choices before sitting (informally or at the table), or a sit-down occasion for a few friends?

For a party, it is advisable to send out invitations at least two to three weeks in advance and it is best to know how many people are actually coming so that you can plan in advance, although snacks and buffets can usually be made to stretch, within limits. With the numbers sorted, you'll know if you need to borrow a tablecloth, plates and/or cutlery for a large crowd.

HERE IS A HANDY CHECKLIST:
• Theme • Invitations • List of foods and drinks to serve • Arrange any special décor needed • Organise borrowed items • Make foods in advance • Make ice • Compile a music playlist • Set up the décor and table settings • Set up the drinks and glasses

CHOOSING THE MENU

When it comes to choosing foods, aim for a good balance of flavours, colours and textures.

People first 'eat with their eyes', so a visually pleasing table or beautifully presented plate of food will make your offerings all the more tempting. There are so many colourful fruits and vegetables that you don't have to try very hard to create eye-catching combinations. Think of green and purple salads, colourful red, orange and green roasted or stir-fried vegetables, fresh herbs to garnish and beautiful berries.

For textures, try to achieve a mix of fresh, light and rich, and crispy and crunchy. Avoid overdoing one type of food, for instance starting with a pastry, followed by a pie and ending with a tart or heavy sponge! Such starch overload will leave your guests feeling bloated.

It's advisable to incorporate a simple variety of foods, especially when doing snacks or buffets, to include meat and/or fish, something vegetarian and a starch-free dish, to cater for most tastes.

For larger parties, start the food preparation a day or two in advance, leaving less to the last minute. Foods that require slow-cooking, setting or freezing are ideal, ready to turn out on the day. Generally, using foods in season will result in fresher, tastier and more economical dishes than out-of-season produce.

Make plenty of ice a few days ahead, depending on freezer space. Fill plastic bags with ice blocks for drinks, and freeze water in plastic food containers for keeping bottles and cans cool on the day.

SET-UP

Let's start with basic table settings. This is very much a personal preference, but generally keep the table décor simple, with no more than two or three colours (white can be one of them). A plain cloth, with a different colour overlay or runner on top, will allow colourful foods to be the central attraction.

For snacks, finger foods and buffets, place the table so that your guests can walk round it, to avoid queues .... a bottle-neck should only be encountered with a drink inside it! Stack plates up at one end of the table, then place the dishes of food so that they are all easily accessible from both sides. Ensure that any sauces or dressings are close to the dishes they accompany.

For informal buffets, put the cutlery and napkins at the other end of the serving table, with cutlery rolled up in napkins, if you like, for easier handling.

Position the drinks table away from the food, to avoid collisions. Fill a wine bucket with ice and chilled white wine or bubbly, otherwise cool the drinks in advance. Ensure that there are glasses, water jugs and cold drinks on offer as an alternative to alcohol. Include bottle openers and slices of lemon, if needed.

For a sit-down party, make sure that there's a place setting for each guest, with cutlery laid for each course, starting from the outer edges for the starters, to the middle for mains, with dessertspoons laid across the top. Position glasses for drinks to the top right-hand side of each setting, and side plates with napkins to the left side of the setting, if using.

FINISHING TOUCHES

For snacks and finger foods, a taller centrepiece in the middle of the table creates an interesting feature; it can either be for decoration only, if space allows, such as a vase of flowers or candlesticks, or it can be eye-catching and serve a purpose, to display a beautiful dish of food on a stand, surrounded by lower dishes around it. For a sit-down meal, a table centrepiece should be low enough for the guests to see each other across the table.

When using flowers or candles, make sure they're not highly scented. Not only will the scent make your guests feel 'heady', or possibly cause allergic reactions, but it will interfere with the aroma of the food. Smell is an important part of tasting flavours. Rather knock your guests out with your stunning food.

Here are some simple yet effective ideas, if you're not having a themed party:

- Use a shallow glass bowl in the centre of the table, with flower heads, or tealight candles for evening parties, floating in water.
- Alternatively, place single stems of flowers in vases or bottles down the middle of the table. Or use candles in glass jars or bottles on the table, for evening parties.
- Scatter lavender stems or one colour of rose petals on a plain tablecloth, for the simplest effect.
- Instead of flowers, use prepared crudités, such as sugar snap peas with thin sticks of celery, in a glass or a small flower pot. Baby carrots with their stalks, mixed with heads of cooked asparagus could be used, and these crudités can form part of the starter.
- Fruits, such as lemons and limes in a glass bowl look effective, particularly with a white tablecloth and green or yellow serviettes.

KEY TO ICONS

Preparation time

Cooling time

Makes (liquid)

Marinating time

Drying time

Makes (quantity)

Cooking time

Setting time

Serves (food)

Freezing time

Resting time

Serves (drinks)

7

USEFUL INFORMATION

MEASUREMENTS

In addition to specific weights indicated in the recipes, the general measurements used throughout are:
- 1 cup = 250ml • 4 cups = 1 litre
- 1 tablespoon (Tbsp) = 15ml • 1 teaspoon (tsp) = 5ml

EQUIPMENT

FOR SNACKS AND FINGER FOODS:
- 1 x 24-cup mini muffin tin, for phyllo pastries, mini muffins and mini cupcakes
- 2 x 12-cup patty pan/tin for mini quiches

FOR CHEESECAKES AND BAKING:
- 20cm and 22cm springform tins

GENERAL USE:
- Hand and electric whisk, stick blender, jug blender
- Ramekins, various serving platters/dishes, dip bowls
- Heatproof glass bowls, kitchen scale, measuring cups and spoons, baking mat, baking paper, clingfilm, kitchen paper

STORE CUPBOARD/FREEZER IDEAS

CUPBOARD:
Olive oil, canola oil, cooking oil spray, soy sauce, lemons, limes, flaked almonds, pecan nuts, sesame seeds, pumpkin seeds, sunflower seeds, stock powders (chicken, beef, vegetable), gelatine, dried herbs, spices, canned tomatoes, tomato paste, red and white wine vinegars, balsamic vinegar, coconut milk/cream, Dijon mustard, English mustard (either powdered or prepared), honey, Tabasco, canned tuna, red onions, white onions, dried rice vermicelli, black olives, capers, chickpeas

FRIDGE:
Garlic, ginger, chilli, cucumber, baby tomatoes, cheeses, fresh herbs, eggs, avocados

FREEZER:
Shelled and deveined prawns, flavoured butters

CHEF'S TRICKS AND TIPS

When searing meat in a pan, use the pan juices and scrapings for the sauce. They are essential in adding taste and help to thicken the sauce naturally. They give that 'umami' (yummy savoury) taste. Allow meat to rest after cooking, so that the juices can be reabsorbed, making the meat more tender and succulent. Keep it covered in a warm place, until needed.

To add smooth tomato to dishes, cut a large tomato in half around the middle and grate it until you reach the skin.

For best results in baking, bring chilled ingredients back to room temperature. Once the ingredients are mixed, bake immediately in a preheated oven. To make it easier to remove baked goods from springform tins, cut the lining paper a little larger (about 5mm) than the base, pressing the extra amount up around the sides. To serve, peel the paper downwards and hold firmly while sliding the item onto a serving dish.

OF INTEREST

USING GELATINE

Gelatine is an animal product and therefore not suitable for vegetarians. Alternative products are available as substitutes, but are used differently to gelatine (not covered here).
- 1 tsp/5ml gelatine powder = 1½ gelatine leaves
- 1 Tbsp/15ml gelatine powder = 4½ gelatine leaves

To dissolve gelatine leaves, soak them in cold water for 5 minutes, remove and squeeze out the water. Thereafter add to hot (not boiling) liquid. To prepare powdered gelatine, sprinkle it into cold liquid until it swells, then heat the liquid (without boiling) to dissolve.

Too much sugar or lemon juice will make gelatine less firm. If you are putting fresh fruits into jelly, avoid pineapple, kiwi, figs and papaya, all of which contain enzymes that inhibit the setting of the jelly.

HERBS AND SPICES

Herbs and spices are used to enhance the taste of a dish, and often its aroma as well. As they can be very strong, a little goes a long way. Dried herbs are generally more concentrated and intense in flavour than fresh herbs, and, as a guide, 1 tsp/5ml of dried herbs is equivalent to 1 Tbsp/15ml of fresh herbs, or a small to medium sprig.

The choice and number of herbs used is very much a personal choice, and best kept to a minimum, in order to distinguish the flavours. Garlic and onion, however, make a good base for many different dishes, and can be delicious mixed with herbs and spices.

There are plenty of wonderful herbs to use, but the following are probably the most widely used in everyday cooking:

- basil, strong aromatic, good with tomato-based dishes.
- bay leaves (use dried, not fresh), enhance the flavour and aroma of meat or fish dishes, especially in slow cooking. Always remove at the end of cooking.
- dill, delicate feathery garnish, strong aroma, for chicken or fish.
- garlic and onion, go with any meats.
- marjoram, subtle for chicken or beef.
- origanum, lemon flavour, for any meat, especially with chicken.
- parsley, subtle and light, for chicken, fish (and any dish to counteract the smell of a lot of garlic!).
- rosemary, strong pine flavour and aroma, for any meat, especially lamb.
- sage, subtle lemon/pine, for chicken or pork.
- tarragon, aniseed flavour, for any meat or fish, and used in Béarnaise sauce.
- thyme, peppery pine and slightly minty flavour and aroma, useful for any meat.

A FEW OF THE MORE FREQUENTLY USED SPICES:

- cayenne pepper comes from red chillies and, if used in moderation, gives warmth to delicate dishes. Goes well with salmon or trout.
- cinnamon, sweetish all-rounder, for savoury and sweet dishes.
- cloves, strong aroma, pungent warming taste, for sweet or savoury dishes.
- coriander, the seeds impart a subtle citrus, warm and woody flavour to all types of meat. The leaves are fragrant, fresh and lemony, for meat and fish, and can be used as garnish.
- cumin, delicate aroma, complements sweetness in meat and vegetables.
- ginger, punchy and zesty, for sweet or savoury dishes. Good with pork.
- mixed spice, mainly used in sweet baking, comprising a mixture of mainly cinnamon, cloves or allspice, ginger.
- paprika, adds warmth and a smoky flavour.

WINE AND FOOD PAIRING

This is one approach. As you become familiar with your wines, you will develop your own preferences and ideas. As a simplistic guide, think of wine as having a personality among food friends. In general:

Match the weights of the wine to the foods. Full-bodied wine goes with heavy, rich food. Delicate wine goes with delicate, light food.

Match the intensity of flavours of the wine with the foods. For example, rieslings, intense in flavour, go with strong intense food flavours. Chardonnays, light in flavour, go with less intense food flavours.

The wine should be slightly more acidic than the acidity in the food. This is especially true of tomatoes, citrus or vinegar in sauces. Highly acidic wine also cuts through fatty or oily foods and sauces. For instance, Italian red wines, high in acid, go with olive oil sauces. Deep red wines, high in tannin, also go well with fats.

The wine should be at least as sweet as the sweetness of the food, especially for desserts. Sweet wines also go well with salty foods, such as cheese.

If you know the wine personality well, bring out its best features with similar food – spicy wines with spicy foods, fruity wines with fruity desserts, creamy/buttery oak-aged wines with creamy/buttery sauces.

On any occasion, a welcoming drink is essential as guests arrive. The simplest and easiest to serve is to have a jug of something at the ready, especially if it's a large party. In addition to alcohol-laden drinks, have an interesting jug of water with herbs and/or fruits or a mocktail available.

For extra visual appeal, have a little bowl of unsprayed herbs and edible flowers to garnish drinks, such as rosemary, lemon thyme, mint, borage flowers (starflower), violets, lavender, pansies or dianthus flowers. Remember that some flowers are toxic and, if in doubt, it's advisable to use only flowers that you can buy from supermarket fresh salad and herb shelves.

To make ice cubes with an edible flower inside, simply wash and place a flower face down in each cup of an ice tray. Half fill with water and freeze. Then top up with more water and freeze again.

Some favourites are included here with non-alcoholic alternatives, to get the party in a festive spirit.

Quantities given are per glass (except for Sangria, Pimms and the sparkling wine cocktails, which use a bottle), so simply multiply quantities if you would like to have jugs at the ready.

To 'muddle' fruits or herbs means to gently crush them, perhaps with the end of a large wooden spoon, to release the oils and flavours. If you don't have a cocktail shaker, use a jar or a sports water bottle, or a blender.

Most of the recipes need crushed ice. Some of the recipes require a simple sugar syrup. This can be made well in advance and stored chilled in the fridge.

RAISING THE SPIRITS

SANGRIA

10 m   10–12

This is delightfully refreshing, but more potent than you think, and will either bring back sweet memories or make a few new ones.

1 apple, rinsed, cored, quartered and sliced
1 orange, rinsed, quartered, sliced and pips removed
⅓ cup brandy
⅓ cup sugar

1 bottle dry red wine
2 cups lemonade (or 1 cup lemonade and 1 cup soda water)
a pinch of ground cinnamon

1. Place the fruit in a large (2-litre) jug. Add the remaining ingredients and mix well. Add plenty of ice and stir.

PIMMS

12–15 m   10–12

Think of Wimbledon, and hot sunny days ... Pimms is like fruit salad in a gin-based, refreshing drink.

2 oranges, rinsed, quartered, sliced and pips removed
¼ cucumber, rinsed and thinly sliced
5–10 strawberries (or other berries of your choice), rinsed, hulled and halved

10–12 small sprigs fresh mint
2 cups Pimms
6 cups lemonade (or mix lemonade with ginger ale)

1. Put the fruit and mint in a large (3-litre) jug or glass dispenser. Pour in the Pimms and lemonade. Stir and add plenty of ice.
2. To serve, pour into long glasses, ensuring each glass has some fruit, a sprig of mint and blocks of ice.

SIMPLE SUGAR SYRUP

 2 m 5 m 1 h 1½ c

1 cup water
1 cup white sugar

1. Heat the water and sugar in a saucepan, and stir to dissolve the sugar. Bring to the boil and simmer for 2 minutes, then remove from the heat and leave to cool. This will keep in a jar in the fridge for at least a month.

ROSE PETAL SYRUP

2 m 5 m 1 h 1½ c

1. Make up the Simple Sugar Syrup (above), adding petals from 4–6 rinsed, organic single-colour roses at the beginning, to infuse the flavour. The resulting colour of the syrup will be a pale version of the colour of petals chosen.
2. Allow the mixture to cool. The longer you leave the petals in the syrup, the more intense the flavour will be. Taste and check the flavour and, when you're satisfied, strain the syrup into a jar and refrigerate for up to 1 week.
3. As an alternative, use bottled rose petal syrup and vary the quantity required in the recipe, according to the desired colour and intensity of flavour.

PINK ROSE PETAL PROSECCO

7–8

⅓ cup pink Rose Petal Syrup (page 12, using dark pink rose petals)
1 x 750ml bottle Prosecco (or any dry sparkling white wine), chilled
pink rose petals, rinsed, for garnishing

1. Divide the syrup among 7–8 glasses. Top up with the Prosecco and
   add 2–3 pink rose petals to each glass.

SPARKLE
with BLACKBERRIES and ROSEMARY

6

1 x 750ml bottle dry sparkling white wine
18–24 blackberries (or blueberries)
6 small sprigs fresh rosemary

1. Divide the wine among 6 glasses. Add 3 or 4 blackberries and a sprig of
   rosemary to each glass.

ROSY GIN COCKTAIL

2 Tbsp gin
2 tsp pink Rose Petal Syrup (page 12)
¼ cup tonic water
½ cup soda water
1 small strip orange zest

1. Pour the gin and syrup into a highball glass. Add a few ice cubes and top up with the tonic and soda water. Gently squeeze the zest oil into the glass, then drop in the zest itself.

Mocktail: Omit the gin and tonic water, increase the Rose Petal Syrup to 1 Tbsp and the soda water to ¾ cup.

GIMLET FIZZ COCKTAIL

2 Tbsp gin
2 tsp lime cordial
2 tsp Simple Sugar Syrup (page 12)
¾ cup sparkling water
1 slice fresh lime

1. Pour the gin, lime cordial and syrup into a highball glass. Add a few ice cubes, then top up with the sparkling water. Drop in the slice of lime.

Mocktail: Omit the gin and Simple Sugar Syrup and increase the lime cordial to 1 Tbsp.

PIÑA COLADA COCKTAIL

4 Tbsp white rum
4 Tbsp coconut cream
½ cup pineapple juice
1 wedge of pineapple for garnishing

1. Shake the liquid ingredients together in a cocktail shaker with some ice. Pour into a highball glass and garnish with the pineapple on the rim of the glass.

Mocktail: Omit the rum.

RASPBERRY MOJITO COCKTAIL

3 fresh mint leaves
½ lime, cut into 2 wedges
2 Tbsp white rum
sparkling water
2 fresh basil leaves and
fresh raspberries for garnishing

1. Muddle the mint leaves and lime in a highball glass. Pour in the rum over some crushed ice. Mix and top up with the sparkling water. Garnish with the basil leaves and raspberries.

Mocktail: Omit the rum.

BLOODY MARY
COCKTAIL

4 Tbsp vodka
½ cup tomato juice
1 tsp lemon juice
¼ tsp Worcestershire sauce
¼ tsp celery salt
2 drops Tabasco sauce
1 stick celery or twist of lemon for garnishing

1. Mix the vodka, tomato juice and lemon juice in a highball glass with some ice. Stir in the Worcestershire sauce, celery salt and Tabasco. Garnish as desired.

Mocktail (Virgin Mary): Omit the vodka.

STRAWBERRY DAIQUIRI
COCKTAIL

3 Tbsp white rum
2 Tbsp fresh lime juice
1 Tbsp strawberry juice
1 strawberry for garnishing

1. Shake the liquid ingredients together in a cocktail shaker with some ice. Pour into a martini glass and garnish with the strawberry on the rim of the glass.

Mocktail: Omit the rum and increase the strawberry juice to 2 Tbsp.

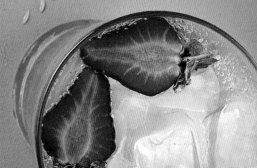

SAUCES, BUTTERS AND RELISHES

HOME-MADE
MAYONNAISE

This is very quick and easy to make, either 2–3 minutes with a stick blender, or 6–10 minutes with a whisk, and is so much more special than readymade mayonnaise. It can be stored in a jar in the fridge for up to 2 weeks. It is essential for the eggs to be at room temperature, and to use an oil that is not watery thin, otherwise the mayonnaise won't thicken. Adding a little olive oil is a safe option, but as olive oil generally has a strong taste, do not use too much.

STICK-BLENDED MAYONNAISE

1 egg
¼ tsp English mustard
1 tsp white spirit vinegar
2 tsp lemon juice
a pinch of salt
1 cup oil (canola with 1 Tbsp olive oil is best)

1. Make the mayonnaise directly in a jar, if you have one with a wide enough opening, or use a jug or a bowl with high sides, to avoid splashes.
2. Carefully crack the egg into the jar and then add the remaining ingredients. Place the stick blender blade over the egg yolk and blend for 20 seconds. Gently lift the blender stick up and down within the jar, for about 1 minute, to emulsify evenly and thicken the mayonnaise.

HAND-WHISKED MAYONNAISE

2 egg yolks
¼ tsp English mustard
1 tsp white spirit vinegar
2 tsp lemon juice
a pinch of salt
1 cup oil (canola with a touch of olive oil is best)

1. Put the yolks into a large mixing bowl, then add the mustard, vinegar, lemon juice and salt. Using either a hand whisk or an electric whisk, beat until the mixture starts to thicken.
2. Gradually drizzle in the oil and continue whisking until the texture is thick and creamy.

FLAVOURED MAYONNAISE Add any of the following to 1 cup of mayonnaise:
Garlic mayonnaise: 2–3 cloves (3–4 tsp) finely chopped garlic, or to taste, for a delicious sauce to go with plain meat or fish, potato wedges, baked potatoes or as a dip.
Coriander or rocket mayonnaise: ½ cup destalked and chopped fresh coriander or rocket.
Herb mayonnaise: 2 Tbsp chopped fresh rosemary, thyme or any other herbs of your choice.
Harissa mayonnaise: 2 Tbsp Harissa Paste (page 114).

FRENCH DRESSING

 5 m　　 ½ c

1 tsp English mustard　　3 Tbsp white wine vinegar
1½–2 tsp sugar　　6 Tbsp oil
a pinch each of salt and pepper　　½ clove garlic, crushed (optional)

1. Shake in a jar to mix well.

HOLLANDAISE AND BÉARNAISE SAUCES

 4 m   8–10 m   ¾ c

This simplified version of hollandaise sauce is so useful and easy that it is worth repeating from *Help! There's a Stove in my Kitchen*. It serves many purposes, from breakfast eggs Benedict, to starters with asparagus, and as a sauce with fish or beef. The quickest way to convert the basic hollandaise to a Béarnaise sauce is to mix in 1 Tbsp of dried tarragon at the end.

2 egg yolks 2 tsp lemon juice
1 tsp white vinegar* 125g cold butter, cubed

1. Place the egg yolks, vinegar, lemon juice and 1 cube of butter in a heatproof bowl, and place over a small saucepan of simmering water. Whisk until the egg yolks thicken and become creamy, while gradually adding the rest of the butter, whisking in after each addition. (Remove from the heat if the eggs look as if they are starting to scramble, and continue whisking in the butter until the mixture is thick and creamy.)
2. Pour into a bowl and set aside to cool. Serve at room temperature.

*For a slightly more acidic taste,
add 1 extra tsp of white vinegar.

PORT AND RED WINE STOCK SAUCE

5–10 m   1½ h   2 c

This sauce goes well with red meat dishes. An added benefit is that a stew can be made from the meat and vegetables.

3 Tbsp oil
3 large slices beef shin on marrow bone
2 medium onions, peeled and sliced
1 clove garlic, peeled and smashed
2 Tbsp balsamic vinegar

½ cup Port (or Cape Ruby or Cape Tawny)
½ cup red wine
1 large carrot, peeled and sliced
1 small sprig of rosemary or thyme
3 cups strong chicken stock

1. Heat the oil in a medium saucepan over a medium to high heat, then sear the meat on both sides, about 7 minutes per side. Remove and scoop out the marrow into the saucepan, but set the meat aside. Reduce the heat to medium and fry the onions with the marrow for 4 minutes, turning to brown in the meat juices. Add the garlic and cook for a further minute.

2. Pour in the vinegar and simmer for 2 minutes, then add the Port and wine, stirring occasionally, until reduced by half.

3. Add the carrot, rosemary or thyme and stock, then bring to the boil, stirring to scrape in the pan juices. Reduce the heat to very low and simmer, with the lid slightly askew, for about 1 hour to reduce the sauce by half, checking the liquid levels occasionally. Add in any pan juices from the roast meat (pouring off excess oils and fat) you might have prepared. Strain the sauce, check the seasoning and serve hot.

NOTE: To make a beef stew using the vegetables, chop the seared beef shin into smaller pieces and place in a saucepan with the strained vegetables. Add 1 x 400g can chopped tomatoes and 2 cups beef stock. Bring to the boil and simmer over very low heat for 2–2½ hours until the meat is tender.

BASE FOR FLAVOURED BUTTER

10+ m   ±100g

It's always useful to make some flavoured butters in advance. Rolled into sausage shapes and wrapped in clingfilm, they can be stored in the freezer ready for any occasion, to serve with grilled steak, chicken, lamb chops or fish, or slotted into an almost-sliced-through French loaf, for instant flavouring.

100g butter, softened to room temperature
flavouring of your choice (see below)

1. Combine the butter with your chosen flavouring in a mixing bowl. Stretch a piece of clingfilm over a chopping board, label a small piece of greaseproof paper (about 10 x 15cm), with the name and place the written-side down on the clingfilm. Spoon the mixture into the middle of the paper and roll into a sausage shape in the paper. Roll the clingfilm around, securing each end with a twist. Place in the freezer until needed.

Anchovy and sun-dried tomato butter: finely chop or crush 4 anchovy fillets and 1 Tbsp chopped sun-dried tomatoes with a pestle and mortar.

Garlic and chilli butter: cut 1–2 red chillies in half lengthways, remove the seeds, and finely chop. Add 1 clove garlic, peeled and finely chopped.

Garlic and parsley butter: combine 2 cloves garlic, peeled and finely chopped, with 2 Tbsp finely chopped fresh parsley.

Herb butter: 2 Tbsp fresh chopped herbs such as rosemary, thyme, origanum and parsley.

Blue cheese butter: 100g crumbled blue cheese melted in 2 Tbsp cream, simmer for 2–3 minutes until thickened, then leave to cool.

CARAMELISED ONIONS

10 m   **45 m**   **1 c**

These can be stored in a jar in the fridge for a few days.
Use as a relish or as an ingredient in tart fillings.

1 Tbsp oil
3 large red onions, peeled and thinly sliced
2 Tbsp balsamic vinegar
1 tsp sugar
salt to taste

1. Heat the oil in a large frying pan over a medium to low heat. Add the onions and gently fry, stirring occasionally for 10 minutes, until softened. Stir in the vinegar, sugar and a good pinch of salt. Cover and cook over a very low heat for 35 minutes, stirring occasionally. Check the seasoning and leave to cool.

NOTE: As a variation, try a balsamic vinegar infused with figs or dates instead of adding sugar.

CHILLI TOMATO RELISH

10 m · **25 m** · **1½ c**

This relish complements meat dishes such as burgers, meatballs or sausages.
It can also be used as a dip.

10g butter
1 Tbsp oil
1 large red onion, peeled and finely chopped
1 clove garlic, peeled and finely chopped
1 small red chilli, deseeded and finely chopped

1 Tbsp red wine vinegar
1 tsp sugar
1 x 400g can whole Italian plum tomatoes
   in juice
2 Tbsp water

1. Melt the butter with the oil in a frying pan over a medium to low heat. Add the onion and fry for 3 minutes until softened. Stir in the garlic, chilli, vinegar and sugar. Mash in the tomatoes and water. Bring to the boil and simmer over a very low heat for 20 minutes, stirring occasionally, until it turns into a flavoursome, chunky tomato sauce.
2. Remove from the heat and leave to cool. Store in a large jar in the fridge.

SNACKS AND FINGER FOODS

For drinks and snacks parties (with no other meal to follow), allow at least 10–12 food bites per person, with a few extra for uncertain numbers. It is better to be generous than to under cater. Keep the snacks bite-size, where possible, so that guests don't have to worry about spilling food on themselves or on the floor.

For cold snacks, prepare everything before your friends arrive, so that the foods can be brought out in relays, when needed. With hot snacks, the preparation should be done in advance, then simply cook or heat the foods at intervals, so that they can be served warm, as needed. Because this will distract you from your guests, it's best to keep hot snacks to a minimum, unless help is available.

To 'dress up' savoury dishes without too much fuss, use herbs and micro herbs, small edible flowers, toasted nuts or seeds, cucumber or carrot ribbons (made by slicing thin strips with a vegetable peeler). For a professional finish, pipe creamy fillings onto blinis, pastries or cucumber rounds with a rose decorating nozzle. If you're looking for a gluten-free alternative to filled phyllo baskets or blinis, use slices of cucumber topped with the same fillings.

For sweet dishes, use edible flowers, pomegranate seeds, toasted nuts, chocolate shapes and sliced fruits.

Serve a selection of crudités, such as sliced matchsticks of raw carrots, cucumber, celery, red pepper, whole baby sweetcorn or sugar snap peas on a platter to go with bowls of dips, or serve the crudités upright in a dip in glasses. The dips also pair well with home-made Flat Breads (page 134) or warmed pita breads, cut into 8 wedges for scooping.

1 x 400g can chickpeas	1 tsp ground cumin
1 large clove garlic, peeled and roughly chopped	½ tsp salt
1 Tbsp tahini	2 Tbsp olive oil in a jug
2 Tbsp lemon juice	paprika for sprinkling

1. Drain the chickpeas into a bowl, reserving half the liquid. Rinse the chickpeas, reserve a few as garnish, then put the rest into a blender with the garlic, tahini, lemon juice, cumin, salt and the reserved liquid from the can. Switch on the blender and drizzle in the oil, until the mixture is smooth, thick and creamy.
2. Serve in a dipping bowl and sprinkle with paprika and a drizzle of oil. Garnish with the reserved chickpeas.

BEETROOT DIP

10 m   10–12

400g cooked beetroot
1 large clove garlic, peeled and roughly chopped
1 cup Greek yoghurt
½ cup crumbled feta cheese
1 Tbsp lemon juice

1 Tbsp olive oil
½ tsp salt
freshly ground black pepper to taste
extra Greek yoghurt and crumbled feta cheese for serving (optional)

1. Blitz all the ingredients in a blender until smooth.
2. Serve in a dipping bowl, along with a dollop of yoghurt swirled on top or feta cheese crumbled over.

BABA GANOUSH
(BRINJAL DIP)

10 m   30 m   6–8

3 Tbsp oil
2 medium brinjals, halved lengthways
1 large clove garlic, whole and unpeeled
1 Tbsp tahini

1 Tbsp lemon juice
½ tsp ground cumin
a small pinch of cayenne pepper

1. Preheat the oven to 200°C. Drizzle a baking tray with 1 Tbsp of the oil.
2. Place the halved brinjals cut-side down on the tray, rubbing in the oil, then add the garlic to the tray. Drizzle over another tablespoon of the oil and roast in the oven for 30 minutes, until softened.
3. When slightly cooled, scoop out the brinjal flesh and squeeze out the garlic clove. Blitz in a blender or mash, together with the tahini, lemon juice, cumin and remaining tablespoon of oil. Season to taste and add the cayenne pepper.
4. Serve in a dipping bowl. Garnish as desired.

ARTICHOKE DIP

10 m   6–8

1 x 390g can artichoke hearts, drained and roughly chopped
1 clove garlic, peeled and roughly chopped
½ cup cream cheese
2 Tbsp mayonnaise
1 jalapeño chilli, roughly chopped
1 sprig of fresh parsley, chopped, for garnishing

1. Blitz all the ingredients, except the parsley, in a blender. Season to taste.
2. Transfer to a dipping bowl, garnish with the parsley and drizzle with olive oil if you like.

TAPENADE

(BLACK OLIVE DIP)

10 m   6 m   6–8

200g pitted black olives (drained weight)
1 Tbsp capers
3 anchovies
1 clove garlic, peeled and roughly chopped

1 Tbsp lemon juice
3 Tbsp olive oil
1 small onion, peeled
1 Tbsp butter

1. Blitz all the ingredients, except the onion and butter, in a blender.
2. Cut off the stalk and root from the onion, then cut in half from stalk to root end. Heat the butter in a small frying pan over a medium to low heat. Place the onion halves cut-side down in the pan, cover and gently fry for 5–6 minutes, until slightly softened and the edges have browned. Remove from the pan and separate the onion petals.
3. Serve the tapenade in a dipping bowl and garnish with the seared onion petals.

29

RICE PAPER SPRING ROLLS

45 m   10 m   24

These are beautiful and delicious, suitable for finger food parties or as a starter.

50g rice vermicelli
12 rice papers
a large handful of fresh coriander
24 cooked prawns, halved lengthways
1 large carrot, peeled and cut into matchsticks
¼ long cucumber, deseeded and cut into matchsticks
½ red pepper, cut into matchsticks
6 spring onions, trimmed and quartered lengthways
4 Tbsp sweet chilli sauce
2 Tbsp chopped fresh chives or edible flowers
for garnishing

DIPPING SAUCE
2 tsp castor sugar
¼ cup cold water
4 tsp fish sauce
2 Tbsp lime juice
1 small red chilli, deseeded and finely chopped
2 Tbsp torn fresh coriander

1. Cook or soak the rice vermicelli according to the packaging instructions, until softened, but still al dente. Drain and leave to cool.
2. Pour warm (but not boiling hot) water into a large frying pan. Immerse a rice paper in the water to soften for a few seconds then place on a board. Approximately 5cm from the bottom edge of the rice paper, arrange 2 sprigs of coriander along the length of the paper, leaving a 5cm margin on either side. Top with 2 prawn halves, 4 sticks each of carrot, cucumber and red pepper, and 2 lengths of spring onion. Place 1 tsp rice vermicelli on top and drizzle 1 tsp sweet chilli sauce over.
3. Fold in the left and right sides of the rice paper, then tightly roll the rice paper up over the filling, compacting the filling, and continue rolling up like a cigar, almost to the top. Place extra coriander and a few chives or edible flowers inside the final turn of the paper. Cut in half at a slight angle, and arrange on a platter. Repeat with the remaining rice papers, then cover with clingfilm. Chill until ready to serve.
4. For the dipping sauce, mix all the ingredients together, stirring well to dissolve the sugar.

ANTIPASTO PLATTER

15 m   6–8

This is a simple and eye-catching selection of readymade cold meats, pâté and a few extras to go with them, arranged on one large platter or board. A fresh French loaf pairs well with all of these elements and can be sliced or left whole for guests to tear off their own pieces.

250g thinly sliced salami
250g thinly sliced ham or seared beef or other cold meats of your choice
100g pâté (your choice)
green and black olives
Marinated Mushrooms (page 142)

Caramelised Onion (page 24)
1 x 280g jar red peppers or Peppadews
marinated artichokes
baby tomatoes
wholegrain mustard
1 fresh long French loaf

CHEESE PLATTER

15 m

Most people love cheese so this is a must-have for parties. Use a large board or platter dish and arrange a variety of cheeses, to include different textures — solid, creamy and soft. A home-made Spinach and Avocado Cheesecake (page 38) also makes an impressive addition to a cheese platter.

Cheddar (or any other hard cheese)	a bunch of grapes or figs (whatever is in season)
Brie or Camembert	some preserves
blue cheese	onion marmalade
herby cream cheese	baby tomatoes
or goat's milk cheese	French bread or savoury biscuits

PARMESAN CRISPS

 6 m 6–8 m 10 m 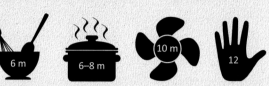 12

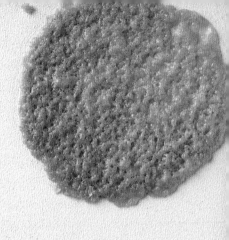

These are delicious on their own, or topped with a dollop of cream cheese, to go with drinks. Alternatively, arrange them over the tops of soups or vegetables to add crunch, or serve them with a creamy dish such as a savoury pannacotta. To vary the flavour, add black pepper, chilli flakes, seeds or herbs before baking.

1 cup finely grated fresh Parmesan or pecorino (avoid powdered, pre-grated cheese)

1. Preheat the oven to 200°C. Line 2 baking trays with ungreased baking paper.
2. Using 1 heaped tablespoon of cheese per crisp, place 6 mounds of the cheese onto each baking tray, flattening the mounds into roughly 7cm rounds, spaced about 5cm apart (to allow for spreading during baking). Bake for 6–8 minutes, until lightly golden, and still soft. Remove from the oven and leave to cool for 10 minutes, to become crisp and firm, before removing them from the paper with a spatula onto a sheet of kitchen paper.
3. The crisps may be stored for 2 days in an airtight food bag or container.

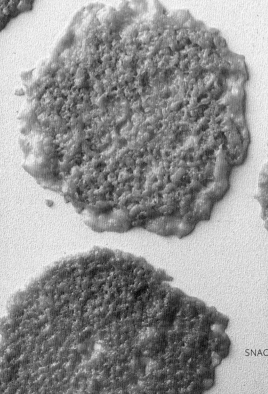

HERB CHEESE TRUFFLES

10–15 m   16

Rustle up these truffles quickly, to go with drinks, or add them to salads or a cheese platter. There is no cooking involved.

2 x 100g logs goat's milk cheese or cream cheese with chives

2 Tbsp chopped fresh parsley

2 Tbsp chopped fresh chives

1 Tbsp chopped fresh basil

1 small red chilli, deseeded and finely chopped

1. Cut each cheese log into 8 pieces and roll the pieces into balls. Mix the herbs and chilli together on a board, then roll the balls in the mixture, coating evenly.
2. Serve with cherry tomatoes on cocktail sticks or on a platter.

BRIE
with FIGS, HONEY and PISTACHIOS

5–10 m   12

This looks beautiful on a dark platter or board, and is effortless to assemble.

1 x 17cm-diameter wheel Brie

8 large ripe figs

1 Tbsp honey

50g unroasted pistachio nuts, roughly chopped (or flaked almonds or mixed seeds, dry-toasted in a pan until lightly browned)

1. Place the Brie on a platter. Cut 4 or 5 of the figs in half, leaving the rest whole. Arrange 2–3 of the halves, cut-side down, randomly on top of the Brie and the rest of the halves on the platter with the whole figs. Drizzle the honey over the Brie, and sprinkle the nuts or seeds on top.

SPINACH AND AVOCADO CHEESECAKE
(NO-BAKE)

30 m   1–5 m   4 h–over-night   8

Suitable for a buffet table or as a cold starter, this beautiful cheesecake can be made a day ahead and simply turned out when needed.

125g savoury crackers
95g butter, melted
1 Tbsp gelatine powder
¾ cup strong vegetable or chicken stock
1 ripe avocado, halved lengthways and pip removed
100g fresh baby spinach, rinsed and thick stalks removed

½ cup crumbled feta cheese
1 clove garlic, peeled and roughly chopped
1 Tbsp lemon juice
1 x 250g pack full-fat cream cheese
1 x 250g tub crème fraîche
a handful of micro herbs for garnishing

1. Lightly spray a 22cm springform cake tin with cooking oil and line with baking paper.
2. Blitz the crackers in a blender or crush them in a mixing bowl with the end of a rolling pin. Mix in the butter, then press the mixture with the back of a spoon into the base of the cake tin. Leave to chill while preparing the filling.
3. Mix the gelatine into the stock. Microwave for 45 seconds to 1 minute (do not boil) to dissolve the gelatine, or stand the cup in hot water and stir until dissolved. Leave to cool for 5 minutes.
4. Scoop the avocado flesh into a blender. Add the spinach, feta, garlic, lemon juice, cream cheese, crème fraîche and stock mixture. Blitz until smooth, intermittently pushing the mixture down with a long spatula. Season and pour over the biscuit base. Chill for at least 4 hours or overnight.
5. When ready to serve, remove from the cake tin (run a thin knife blade around the edge, if necessary), carefully transferring it onto a serving platter. Garnish with a few micro herbs.

FILLED PHYLLO BASKETS

20 m   6–7 m
            + filling   21

These bite-size, pretty little baskets are so versatile as they can be used for the savoury fillings opposite and the sweet fillings below. Because phyllo pastry dries out so quickly, have a large plastic bag or sheet of clingfilm at the ready to cover the pastry while you are working. (I find that a damp tea towel often makes the pastry go wrinkly and unmanageable.)

2 sheets phyllo pastry (36 x 42cm each)*
30g butter, melted

1. Preheat the oven to 180°C. Lightly spray a 24-cup mini muffin tin with cooking oil.
2. Place 1 sheet of phyllo on a large board and brush it with half the melted butter. Place another phyllo sheet on top and brush it with the remaining butter. Cut in half lengthways and place one half over the other to create 4 layers of phyllo. Cut the 4-layer stack into 6cm squares (which will create a total of 21 squares). Press the squares into the prepared muffin cups with the phyllo corners upright.
3. Bake for 6–7 minutes until crispy and slightly golden. Remove from the tray onto kitchen paper and leave to cool. They can be stored in an airtight container for a few days until needed. Once filled with any of the following suggestions, they are best served on the same day.

Don't worry if the phyllo sheets aren't exactly this size, as they vary from brand to brand. Simply follow the same instructions and cut them roughly into 6cm squares, and press into the mini-muffin cups.

SWEET SNACKS
Toasted Macadamia Nut Blondies (page 169).
Lemon Meringue Nests (page 152).

The following make delicious sweet fillings for the phyllo baskets. Remember to fill the baskets just before serving to prevent the pastry from going soggy.
Peeled and chopped pear and broken walnuts. Make a **chocolate ganache** by melting 90g chocolate into ¼ cup cream. Cool slightly, then drizzle the ganache over the pears and walnuts.
Amarula Sabayon (page 155) and top each with a raspberry.

AVOCADO SALSA

1 large ripe avocado, peeled and finely cubed
1 Tbsp fresh lime juice
8 baby tomatoes, finely chopped
3 spring onions, trimmed and finely sliced
a few drops of Tabasco sauce
a handful of fresh coriander leaves, torn

1. Gently mix all the ingredients together, reserving half the coriander. Season to taste, then fill the baskets and garnish with the remaining coriander.

CHICKEN IN HOISIN SAUCE

1½ Tbsp sesame seeds
¼ cucumber, rinsed
1 cup cooked and finely shredded or chopped chicken
¼ cup mayonnaise
1½ Tbsp hoisin sauce
1 tsp soy sauce
½ tsp sesame oil
1 long stick celery, rinsed, leaves removed and finely diced
snipped fresh chives for garnishing

1. Lightly toast the sesame seeds in a dry frying pan over a medium heat for 2–3 minutes.
2. Quarter the cucumber lengthways, cut out the middle core of seeds and discard. Finely dice the cucumber.
3. Mix the chicken, mayonnaise, hoisin sauce, soy sauce, sesame oil, cucumber and celery. Check seasoning, and place a rounded teaspoon of the mixture into each phyllo basket. Garnish with chives and sprinkle with sesame seeds.

SMALL PRAWNS IN BLOODY MARY COCKTAIL SAUCE

You could make this a Virgin Mary filling by omitting the vodka.

¼ cup mayonnaise
1 tsp tomato paste
1 tsp fresh lime juice
¼ tsp Worcestershire sauce
a few drops of Tabasco sauce
1 tsp vodka (optional)
40 peeled and cooked small prawns
1 baby gem lettuce, 2 or 3 outer leaves removed
unsmoked paprika for sprinkling

1. Mix together the mayonnaise, tomato paste, lime juice, Worcestershire sauce, Tabasco sauce and vodka (if using) until well combined.
2. Slice the lettuce, then shred finely. Press a teaspoon of the shreds into the bottom of each pastry basket, dip 2 prawns in the mayonnaise mixture and place on top of each basket. Sprinkle with a little paprika.

SMOKED SALMON OR TROUT MOUSSE WITH FRESH DILL

¾ cup smooth plain cottage cheese
45g smoked salmon or trout ribbons, finely chopped
1 tsp lemon juice
1½ Tbsp snipped fresh chives
a small pinch of cayenne pepper
a handful of micro herbs
1 large sprig of fresh dill for garnishing

1. Combine the cottage cheese, salmon or trout, lemon juice, chives and cayenne pepper. Season to taste. Place a teaspoon of micro herbs in the base of each basket, fill with the cottage cheese mixture and top with dill.

QUICK BLINIS

5 m

15 m
+ topping

25

1 egg
½ cup self-raising flour
½ cup milk
15g butter, melted

1 sprig of fresh dill, chopped (optional)
oil for spraying
oil for frying

1. Lightly whisk the egg in a mixing bowl. Add the flour and half the milk, continue whisking and gradually add the remaining milk until a smooth batter forms. Stir in the butter. Add the dill, if using.
2. Spray a frying pan with cooking oil then swirl in an extra teaspoon of oil. Heat over medium to high heat and, using 2 tsp batter per blini, make 5 blinis at a time. Cook for 1 minute until light-golden underneath and bubbles appear on top. Flip and cook for a further minute until golden-spotted underneath. Transfer to a plate. Reduce the heat if the blinis start browning too quickly.
3. Repeat, swirling in a teaspoon of oil, until all the batter is used. Top with a topping of your choice.

BEETROOT AND CRÈME FRAÎCHE

50g cooked beetroot
½ cup crème fraîche
a pinch of ground cumin
salt and pepper to taste
black sesame seeds or black 'caviar' for garnishing

1. Blitz together the beetroot, crème fraîche, cumin and seasoning. Pipe dollops of the purée onto the blinis and garnish with the sesame seeds or 'caviar'.

CRÈME FRAÎCHE AND SALMON

a dollop of crème fraîche
1 small strip smoked salmon
cayenne pepper to taste
1 sprig of fresh dill for garnishing

1. Top the blini with the crème fraîche followed by the salmon. Season with the pepper and garnish with dill.

AVOCADO-CORIANDER PESTO

30g pecan nuts
1 ripe avocado, peeled and roughly chopped
1 Tbsp lemon juice
1 clove garlic, roughly chopped
30g fresh coriander leaves, large stalks removed
½ mild green chilli, deseeded
2 Tbsp oil
salt and pepper to taste
25 cooked prawns

1. To make the pesto, blitz all the ingredients, except the prawns, in a blender. Place 1 tsp of the mixture onto each blini and top with a prawn.

PULLED PORK AND RED COLESLAW MINI PITAS

12–16 ready-made mini pitas
Pulled Pork in Barbecue Sauce (page 109)
Red Coleslaw Salad (page 137)

1. Fill each pita with some of the pork and the coleslaw.

COCKTAIL STICKS

Although it's traditional to serve many cocktail snacks on cocktail sticks, some of them (such as those on the pages following this) could be left free on a platter, or served on spoons. The choice is yours. Below are some ideas for delicious combinations threaded onto cocktail sticks.

Baby tomatoes, basil leaves and baby mozzarella balls (bocconcini)

Prosciutto, watermelon cubes and feta

Blue cheese cubes with red grapes

Greek salad with baby tomato, feta, cucumber and black olives

Serrano ham, nectarine slices, mozzarella cubes

GLAZED CHIPOLATA SAUSAGES
and DIP

5 m   30 m   24

2 Tbsp oil
24 chipolata sausages, separated
1 Tbsp Dijon mustard
1 Tbsp honey

DIP
15g butter
½ small red onion, finely chopped
1 small clove garlic, peeled and finely chopped
½ x 400g can chopped tomatoes
salt and pepper

1. Preheat the oven to 180°C. Line a baking tray with baking paper.
2. Heat the oil in a large frying pan over a medium heat and fry the sausages in a single layer for 7–8 minutes, turning to brown all over. Remove and set aside.
3. To make the glaze, mix the mustard and honey on a plate. Roll the sausages in the glaze and place on the prepared baking tray in a single layer.
4. For the dip, heat the butter in a small saucepan and gently fry the onion over a medium to low heat for 3 minutes, until softened. Add the garlic and cook for 1 minute, then mash in the tomatoes. Bring to the boil and simmer for 5 minutes until the mixture has slightly reduced. Season to taste and leave to cool.
5. Shortly before serving, heat the sausages in the oven for 10 minutes. Serve hot on cocktail sticks, with the dip.

CHICKEN AND BACON BITES

1 clove garlic, peeled and finely chopped
4 Tbsp plain yoghurt
2 large chicken fillets, trimmed and cut into
20 bite-size cubes

10 rashers streaky bacon, halved
1 Tbsp oil

1. Mix the garlic with the yoghurt and marinate the chicken in the mixture for 30 minutes.
2. Preheat the oven to 180°C and place a rack on a grill pan.
3. Shake any excess marinade from the chicken, and wrap a piece of bacon around each chicken cube. Arrange them on the rack in the grill pan, seam-side down, and bake for 15 minutes, until the chicken is just cooked.
4. Heat the oil in a frying pan over medium heat and fry the cubes for 2–3 minutes on each side until the bacon is crisp. Serve hot, on cocktail sticks.

PRAWN AND CHORIZO BITES

15g butter
24 medium prawns, peeled and deveined
(thawed if frozen)

1 Tbsp fresh lemon juice
2 tsp oil
80g chorizo, cut into 24 thin slices

1. Melt the butter in a frying pan over a medium heat, and fry the prawns for 2–3 minutes, until opaque. Transfer to a bowl, pour over the lemon juice, cover and set aside.
2. Heat the oil in a clean frying pan over a medium heat. Add the chorizo and fry for 2 minutes, turning to brown evenly. Drain on kitchen paper.
3. Thread a prawn and a slice of chorizo onto cocktail sticks, and serve warm.

CHICKEN SATAY

20 m   1 h   20 m   25–30

This could be used as a main course by adding an extra chicken fillet, halving the chicken fillets horizontally and gently cooking the chicken in the sauce for 10—15 minutes, until cooked through. Serve with basmati rice and a salad of cucumber, sliced red onion and fresh coriander leaves.

3 large chicken fillets, trimmed and sliced into strips
4 tsp oil
½ cup water
2 Tbsp chopped fresh coriander leaves

MARINADE
1 tsp mild curry paste
1 small red chilli, deseeded and finely chopped
½ tsp ground cumin
1 clove garlic, peeled and finely chopped
¼ cup smooth peanut butter
2 Tbsp soy sauce
2 Tbsp fresh lime juice
½ cup coconut milk

1. First make the marinade by mixing all the ingredients in a bowl. Add the chicken and coat well. Leave to marinate for at least 1 hour. Before cooking the chicken, shake off the excess marinade into the bowl, and reserve for the dipping sauce.
2. Heat half the oil in a large frying pan over a medium heat and fry half the chicken for 3–4 minutes per side, turning to brown with a lovely crust. Transfer to a dish and wipe the pan with kitchen paper to remove any excess crust. Add the remaining oil to the pan and fry the rest of the chicken.
3. In a small saucepan, mix the leftover marinade with the water, bring to the boil and simmer for 4 minutes until creamy in texture. Pour into a dipping bowl.
4. Sprinkle the coriander over the chicken and serve warm on cocktail sticks with the dipping sauce, and wedges of fresh lime if you like.

THAI CHICKEN MEATBALLS
with CHILLI DIPPING SAUCE

20 m | 20 m | 24

MEATBALLS
500g chicken mince
2 cloves garlic, peeled and grated
1 small red chilli, deseeded and finely chopped
2 spring onions, finely chopped
1 Tbsp fresh lime juice
1 tsp salt
freshly ground black pepper to taste
1 Tbsp oil

GLAZE
2 tsp honey
2 tsp soy sauce

DIPPING SAUCE
4 Tbsp sweet chilli sauce
2 Tbsp fresh lime juice

1. Preheat the oven to 180°C. Line a baking tray with baking paper.
2. For the meatballs, combine the chicken mince, garlic, chilli, spring onions, lime juice, salt and pepper. Shape the mixture into balls, using 1 Tbsp of the mixture per ball and arrange on the prepared tray. Drizzle the oil over and bake for 10 minutes.
3. To make the glaze, mix the honey with the soy sauce and spoon over the meatballs, turning them to glaze all over. Return to the oven and bake for another 5 minutes. Turn the meatballs and bake for a further 5 minutes, until lightly browned. Thread the meatballs onto cocktail sticks and transfer to a serving platter.
4. Mix the sweet chilli sauce with the lime juice to make the dipping sauce. Pour into a small bowl and serve with the meatballs on the platter.

COCONUT-COATED PRAWNS
with HARISSA MAYONNAISE

 30 m 4 m 24

½ cup desiccated coconut
24 large prawns, peeled and deveined (thawed if frozen)
1 egg, lightly beaten
¼ cup oil plus 1 Tbsp extra
6 limes, quartered lengthways

HARISSA MAYONNAISE
1 Tbsp Harissa Paste (page 114 or readymade)
½ cup mayonnaise (page 19 or readymade)

1. First make the harissa mayonnaise by mixing together the Harissa Paste and mayonnaise.
2. Spread the coconut on a plate and season to taste. Dip the prawns in the egg, then roll in the coconut.
3. Heat the 1/4 cup of oil in a large frying pan over a medium to high heat, then fry half the prawns for 1 minute per side, until golden and crispy. Transfer to a plate lined with kitchen paper. Add the extra oil to the pan, reduce the heat slightly and fry the remaining prawns. Drain on kitchen paper.
4. Serve on cocktail sticks with the lime wedges and harissa mayonnaise.

STUFFED JALAPEÑO HALVES

10 m   10 m   10

5 jalapeño chillies
2 Tbsp cream cheese
½ clove garlic, peeled and finely chopped
1 spring onion, trimmed and finely sliced
½ tsp fresh lime juice
¼ cup grated Cheddar cheese

1. Preheat the oven to 200°C. Line a baking tray with baking paper.
2. Cut the jalapeños in half lengthways, scrape out the seeds and discard. Arrange the jalapeños cut-side up on the baking tray.
3. Combine the cream cheese, garlic, spring onion and lime juice, then spoon into the jalapeño cavities, season well and top with the Cheddar cheese. Bake for 10 minutes until sizzling and the cheese has melted. Serve hot.

CHEESEBURGER BALLS

These succulent little balls have melted cheese centres and are quite delicious with a chilli tomato relish.

1½ cups Chilli Tomato Relish (page 25)
500g beef mince
1 clove garlic, peeled and finely chopped
1 Tbsp Dijon mustard
a pinch of chilli powder
70g block Cheddar cheese, cut into 24 cubes
1½ Tbsp oil

1. Preheat the oven to 180°C. Line a baking tray with baking paper.
2. Make the relish and while it's still cooking, mix together the mince, garlic, mustard and chilli powder, add seasoning and mix well. Press a tablespoon of the mixture around a cube of cheese, shape into a ball and place onto the prepared tray. Repeat with the remaining mixture and cheese cubes. Drizzle the oil over the balls and bake for 10 minutes.
3. Transfer the balls to a serving platter and serve immediately while still hot, with the relish on the side.

MINI QUICHES OR FRITTATAS

30 m | 12–14 m + filling | 20

Uncooked quiche pastry cases may be made well in advance, kept in the shallow patty tins (to retain their shape), covered in clingfilm and stored in the fridge or freezer for a few days. If you prefer not to use the pastry, use the fillings to make frittatas instead.

BASIC PASTRY
1 cup cake flour
1 cup finely grated Cheddar cheese
80g cold butter, cubed

BASIC FILLING
3 eggs
¾ cup cream cheese or crème fraîche
1 cup grated Cheddar cheese

1. Brush or spray a little oil over 2 x 12-cup, shallow patty tins (for quiches) or a 24-cup mini muffin tin for frittatas.
2. First prepare the pastry by combining the flour, Cheddar cheese and butter in a food processor for about 90 seconds until the mixture clumps together. Shape the dough into a ball and cut into quarters. Divide each quarter into 5 balls, then press each ball into a cup of the patty tin, lining the base and sides evenly. Refrigerate while preparing the filling. Preheat the oven to 180°C.
3. For the basic filling, whisk the eggs, cream cheese or crème fraîche and grated cheese together, then season with salt and pepper to taste. Spoon a tablespoon of the mixture into each pastry case (or muffin cup if making frittatas). If you are adding one of the following fillings, add it at this point.
4. Bake quiches for 12–14 minutes and frittatas for 12 minutes. Remove from the oven and leave in the tin for 5 minutes before transferring to a platter. Serve warm.

BABY MARROW, RED ONION AND FETA FILLING

15g butter
1 medium red onion, peeled and finely chopped
250g baby marrows, rinsed and finely sliced
garlic and herb seasoning to taste
¼ cup crumbled feta

1. Melt the butter in a frying pan over a medium heat and fry the onion and baby marrows for 3 minutes, until the onion is softened and the marrows are lightly browned at the edges. Sprinkle with garlic and herb seasoning, and salt and pepper.
2. To assemble, for each mini quiche or frittata, gently push 1 heaped teaspoon of the baby marrow mixture into the basic filling. Sprinkle half a teaspoon of feta over the top, then bake.

CHICKEN AND MUSHROOM FILLING

1 small chicken fillet
1 Tbsp oil
175g small button mushrooms, wiped and thinly sliced
1 clove garlic, peeled and finely chopped
a pinch of dried thyme
1 Tbsp soy sauce

1. Trim and chop the chicken into small pieces so that it resembles chunky mince.
2. Heat the oil in a frying pan over a medium heat and fry the chicken, mushrooms, garlic and thyme for 4 minutes. Mix in the soy sauce and season with black pepper to taste.
3. To assemble, for each mini quiche or frittata, gently push 1 heaped teaspoon of the chicken and mushroom mixture into the basic filling before baking.

Continued on following page

ASPARAGUS FILLING

10 fresh asparagus spears, woody ends removed, **or**
1 x 180g jar asparagus spears, drained and cut into
short pieces

1. If using fresh asparagus, cover the base of a wide frying pan with water (no more than 1cm deep) and bring to the boil. Place the asparagus flat in the water, but not submerged to avoid sogginess. Cover the pan and steam over a medium heat for 3–5 minutes until just tender, depending on thickness of the stems. Remove and drain. Cut into short pieces to fit into the pastry cases.
2. To assemble, for each mini quiche or frittata, gently push 2–3 pieces of asparagus into the basic filling before baking.

CARAMELISED ONION AND BLUE CHEESE FILLING

½ cup Caramelised Onion (page 24)
75g blue cheese, crumbled

1. To assemble, for each mini quiche or frittata, gently push 1 tsp each of Caramelised Onion and crumbled blue cheese into the basic filling before baking.

HAM, MUSTARD AND PARMESAN FILLING

1 rounded Tbsp Dijon mustard
100g sliced ham, cut thinly into ribbons
¼ cup finely grated Parmesan

1. Mix the mustard into the basic filling before spooning into the quiches or frittatas. Alternatively, use ½ teaspoon mustard among 3 quiches or frittatas, and swirl into the basic filling when assembling.
2. To assemble, for each mini quiche or frittata, gently push 1 tsp ham and ½ tsp Parmesan into the basic filling before baking.

BLACK OLIVE AND BABY TOMATO FILLING

100g pitted black olives, finely chopped
10 baby tomatoes, halved
10 anchovies, halved (optional)

1. To assemble, for each mini quiche or frittata, gently push 1 tsp chopped olives and half a tomato into the basic filling. If using, place the anchovy half on top, then bake.

SPINACH AND FETA FILLING

½ cup water
175g baby spinach leaves, rinsed
3–4 spring onions, trimmed and sliced
¼ cup crumbled feta

1. Boil the water in a large saucepan and add the spinach. Turn to wilt evenly, for 3–4 minutes, then drain well and squeeze out any excess moisture. Chop finely.
2. To assemble, for each mini quiche or frittata, gently push 2 slices of spring onion and 1 heaped teaspoon of spinach into the basic filling. Sprinkle ½ tsp feta on top, then bake.

TOMATO TART

 10 m 30–35 m 6

This tart* makes a delicious light lunch or addition to a buffet.

1 cup Caramelised Onion (page 24)
1 cup cake flour
1 cup finely grated Cheddar cheese
½ tsp English mustard powder
80g cold butter, cubed
3 large tomatoes, sliced
1 x 100g log goat's milk cheese or cream cheese with herbs
small, fresh basil leaves for garnishing

1. Preheat the oven to 180°C. Lightly grease a shallow, 20cm-diameter ovenproof dish.
2. First prepare the Caramelised Onion (if you don't have it already made), and leave to cool.
3. Mix the flour, Cheddar cheese, mustard and butter in a food processor for about 1½ minutes, until it clumps together in a ball. Press into the base and sides of the prepared dish.
4. Spread the Caramelised Onion over the pastry, then top with an overlapping circle of the tomato slices, with 2 or 3 slices in the centre.
5. Cut rounds of the goat's milk cheese or cream cheese logs and dot them about, on top of the tomatoes. Bake for 30 minutes.
6. Leave to rest for 5 minutes, then scatter over some basil leaves and serve hot.

*If you'd prefer to make small tartlets, adjust the baking time to 15–20 minutes (depending on the size of the tartlets) and place a slice of tomato on top of a round of goat's milk cheese for each tartlet.

EGGS BENEDICT
BREAKFAST 'BASKETS'

5 m   12–18 m   12

cooking oil spray
12 slices ham
12 eggs

2 x quantity Hollandaise Sauce (page 21)
a handful of fresh chives, snipped, for
garnishing (optional)

1. Preheat the oven to 180°C. Spray a 12-cup muffin tin with cooking oil, ensuring that the cups are well greased.
2. Line each muffin cup with a slice of ham. Break an egg over each slice of ham cup, keeping the yolk whole. Bake for 12–15 minutes, until the egg white is just cooked and the yolk still soft. (Cook for 2–3 minutes longer if you prefer hard yolks.)
3. Quickly remove the cooked ham and eggs from the muffin cups to avoid over-cooking, and serve with 1–2 Tbsp Hollandaise Sauce poured over each serving. Top with the chives. As an extra, you could serve the baskets with cooked halved tomatoes. Place the tomato halves cut-side up on a separate baking tray, with a small blob of butter on each. Bake them with the eggs for the same length of time.

TIP: Try not to spill any egg around the ham, to prevent the egg from sticking to the muffin cup.

BAKED CAMEMBERT
and GARLIC BREAD

 15 m 25 m 6

Garlic bread dipped into melting Camembert makes a sumptuous snack.
Alternatively, use crunchy sticks of celery for a starch-free option.

	BAKED GARLIC BREAD
1 small (about 9cm diameter) Camembert	
1 clove garlic, peeled and thinly sliced	2 tsp finely chopped garlic
1 sprig of fresh thyme	3 sprigs fresh parsley, finely chopped
olive oil for drizzling	60g butter, softened
	1 short French loaf (about 40cm long)

1. Preheat the oven to 180°C. Using a fork, mash the garlic and parsley into the butter. Cut diagonal slits into the loaf, about 2cm apart but leave the bottom crust intact. Spread the butter generously into the slits. Wrap the loaf in foil with the opening at the top and fold the ends over at the top and sides. Bake for 25 minutes.
2. Meanwhile, place the Camembert in an ovenproof dish. Make incisions in the top of the cheese and insert slices of the garlic. Top with the thyme and drizzle with the oil. Place in the oven alongside the garlic bread, for 10–15 minutes, or until the cheese starts to melt. Serve with the garlic bread and Caramelised Onion (page 24), if desired.

SOUPS AND STARTERS

GAZPACHO

20 m   4

This is a refreshing cold soup that can be served not only as a starter, but also in large shot glasses for parties or buffets.

1 large cucumber, peeled
1 large red pepper, deseeded and roughly chopped
4 spring onions, trimmed and sliced (but retain a little of the green section)
1 x 400g can chopped and peeled Italian tomatoes
1 cup tomato cocktail
1 clove garlic, chopped
1 small red chilli, deseeded
1 tsp sugar
1 Tbsp balsamic vinegar
1 Tbsp oil
a handful of fresh coriander for garnishing

1. Cut the cucumber in quarters lengthways, and scrape away the seeds. Finely dice a small handful of the cucumber and set aside for garnishing, and chop the rest into chunks. Finely dice a small amount of the red pepper and retain as garnish, and keep the rest roughly chopped.
2. Blitz the chunks of cucumber and red pepper with the spring onions, tomatoes, tomato cocktail, garlic, chilli, sugar, vinegar and oil in a blender for a few seconds, so that the mixture is still a little chunky. Season well, then chill until needed.
3. Serve garnished with the reserved cucumber, red pepper and coriander.

CAULIFLOWER AND ALMOND SOUP

5 m   40 m   4

This soup is delicious hot or cold.

55g ground almonds	500g cauliflower florets, rinsed
35g butter	3 cups strong chicken or vegetable stock
1 small onion, peeled and roughly chopped	¼ cup thin cream
1 clove garlic, peeled and roughly chopped	

1. Toast the almonds in a dry frying pan over a medium heat for 3–5 minutes until they turn golden, shaking the pan often. Remove from the pan and set aside for later use, reserving 1 Tbsp of the toasted almonds as garnish.

2. In a large saucepan, melt the butter over a medium heat and fry the onion and garlic for 3–4 minutes, until softened. Add the cauliflower and stock, bring to the boil, then cover and simmer over low heat for 30 minutes, or until the cauliflower is tender. Leave to cool.

3. Blend the cauliflower with the almonds. Stir in the cream and season to taste. Chill until needed.

4. When ready to serve, gently reheat over a medium to low heat if serving hot. Sprinkle the reserved almonds over each serving, along with any other garnish of your choice.

ROASTED RED PEPPER AND TOMATO SOUP

10 m + 20 m   40 m   4–6

2 Tbsp olive oil

1 large red pepper, deseeded and quartered

12 large plum tomatoes, halved lengthways

1 unpeeled red onion, halved

2 medium cloves garlic, unpeeled

1 tsp dried thyme

1 cup vegetable or chicken stock

1 tsp chopped fresh basil leaves or 1 tsp basil pesto, plus extra for garnishing

½ teaspoon sugar (optional)

½–1 tsp dried chilli flakes

cream for serving (optional)

1. Preheat the oven to 200°C.
2. Drizzle half the olive oil onto a baking tray and arrange the pepper, tomatoes and onion cut-side down, in a single layer, on the tray. Add the garlic, sprinkle with thyme and drizzle with the remaining oil. Season well with salt and pepper. Bake for 40 minutes, then remove from the oven and leave to cool for 10 minutes on the tray.
3. Use tongs to remove and discard the vegetable skins, and squeeze the garlic cloves out of their skins. Scoop the vegetables, herbs and pan juices into a blender. Add the stock, basil, sugar (if using) and chilli flakes. Blitz until fairly smooth. Season to taste.
4. Reheat gently, then serve drizzled with the cream, if using, and a little chopped fresh basil or pesto.

MUSHROOM CAPPUCCINO SOUP
with CIABATTA 'BISCOTTI'

15 m   25 m   4

This soup can be made a day or two in advance, and refrigerated until required. The ciabatta biscotti can be prepared early on the day of serving and kept crisp in an airtight container.

oil for drizzling
½ Italian ciabatta loaf
40g butter
1 medium onion, peeled and finely chopped
1 large clove garlic, peeled and finely chopped
500g mixed mushrooms, wiped and chopped

½ tsp dried thyme
2 cups water
3 Tbsp soy sauce
1 Tbsp lemon juice
½ cup cream

1. Preheat the grill. Drizzle a little oil onto a baking tray.
2. Slice the ciabatta into 3cm-thick slices and cut each slice into 3 or 4 'fingers'. Arrange them on the prepared tray, drizzle with a little more oil and place under the hot grill for 4–5 minutes. Turn the pieces to brown all over, then set aside to cool until needed.
3. Melt the butter in a large, deep frying pan or a wide saucepan, and fry the onion and garlic over medium heat for 4 minutes, stirring occasionally, until the onion is softened. Add the mushrooms and stir-fry for 5–6 minutes until the mushroom juices are released. Add the thyme and water, and bring to the boil. Simmer gently over a low heat for 10 minutes. Cool slightly, then blitz in a blender (or with a stick blender) with the soy sauce and lemon juice until smooth. Return to the pan or saucepan and season to taste.
4. Whip the cream in a separate bowl, until light and fluffy. When ready to serve, reheat the soup gently and pour it into cups with a dollop of the whipped cream on top. Swirl the cream lightly to cover the top of the soup, to make it look like cappuccino froth, and garnish as desired.
5. Serve with 2 of the crispy ciabatta 'biscotti' on each saucer.

BEETROOT AND APPLE SOUP

 10 m 35 m 4–6

A refreshing soup that can be served hot or cold.

30g butter
1 large red onion, peeled and sliced
2 Granny Smith apples, peeled, cored and sliced
1 large clove garlic, peeled and chopped
¼ tsp ground ginger
½ tsp ground cumin
450g cooked beetroot, chopped
4 cups strong chicken or vegetable stock
1 Tbsp lemon juice
½ cup plain yoghurt for serving

1. Melt the butter in a large saucepan over a medium heat and fry the onion for 3 minutes, until softened. Add the apples, garlic, ginger and cumin, cover and allow to sweat for 3 minutes, stirring occasionally.
2. Add the beetroot and stock. Cover and bring to the boil, then simmer over a medium to low heat for 15–20 minutes until the apples and beetroot are soft. Leave to cool slightly, then add the lemon juice and blitz in a blender (or with a stick blender) until smooth. Season to taste and chill until ready to serve.
3. If serving hot, gently reheat the soup over medium to low heat, stirring occasionally. Hot or cold, pour into bowls and swirl in a little of the yoghurt. Garnish as desired.

BASIL PANNACOTTA
with TOMATO AND OLIVE SALSA

 15 m
 5 m
 4 h–over-night
 6

cooking oil spray
1½ gelatine leaves
1 cup cream
30g chopped fresh basil (reserve some for the salsa)
1 cup full-fat plain yoghurt
1 tsp garlic and herb seasoning

SALSA
a few reserved fresh basil leaves
2 medium tomatoes, finely chopped
½ cup olives, pips removed, chopped
2 spring onions, trimmed and sliced
1 Tbsp balsamic vinegar*
2 Tbsp olive oil

1. Lightly spray 6 small ramekins or moulds with cooking oil. Soften the gelatine leaves in a bowl of cold water for 5 minutes.
2. Pour the cream into a saucepan, add the chopped basil and bring almost to the boil, gently over a medium to low heat, then set aside.
3. Squeeze the water from the gelatine leaves and stir them into the cream and basil until they have completely dissolved. Stir in the yoghurt and garlic and herb seasoning. Briefly blitz in a blender until the mixture turns green from the basil. Season to taste, then pour the pannacotta mixture into the prepared ramekins or moulds, cover with clingfilm and chill for at least 4 hours, but preferably overnight.
4. To make the salsa, combine all the ingredients and mix well.
5. Remove the pannacottas from their moulds, using a thin knife to run around the edge, if necessary, onto side plates and top each with a spoonful of the salsa. Serve with crisp Melba toast.

A quick balsamic reduction would be perfect here. First ensure the windows are open. Simply pour ½ cup balsamic vinegar into a small saucepan and bring it to the boil over a medium heat. Turn down the heat and simmer for 5 minutes, to reduce by half. Pour into a cup and allow to cool. This makes a delicious rich finishing touch, to drizzle over the dish. If using the reduction, omit the balsamic vinegar in the salsa and dress with olive oil only.

AVOCADO MOUSSE
with SMALL PRAWNS

15 m   4

This mousse is quick and easy to make and is best served on the same day to prevent the avocado colour from browning. As it is quite rich, a little goes a long way.

2 large ripe avocados, peeled and pips removed
1 Tbsp lemon juice
1 tsp soy sauce
½ tomato, grated

2 tsp mayonnaise
a few drops of Tabasco to taste

TOPPING
1 clove garlic, peeled and grated
1 Tbsp lemon juice
2 Tbsp oil
16–20 cooked, peeled and deveined small prawns
fresh coriander and edible flowers for garnishing

1. Blitz the avocados, lemon juice, soy sauce, tomato, mayonnaise and Tabasco with a stick blender, until smooth. Alternatively, mash with a fork until smooth. Spoon the mousse into 4 ramekins or glasses and chill until needed.

2. For the topping, combine the garlic, lemon juice and oil. Marinate the prawns in the mixture and chill until needed.

3. When ready to serve, top the mousse with the prawns and scatter over the coriander leaves and flowers. Serve with homemade Melba toast (thinly sliced stale white bread, grilled until crisply toasted) or carrot and cucumber sticks.

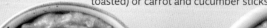

SMOKED TROUT SALAD

10 m   4

1 Tbsp sesame seeds
¼ cup mayonnaise
1 tsp horseradish sauce or ½ tsp wasabi paste
¼ cucumber
80g baby salad greens
150–200g (8 ribbons) smoked trout or salmon
1 Tbsp chopped fresh chives
sprigs of fresh dill for garnishing

DRESSING
1 Tbsp honey
2 Tbsp fresh lime juice
1 tsp soy sauce
2 Tbsp oil

1. Toast the sesame seeds in a dry frying pan over a medium heat, shaking the pan to toast evenly, then remove and set aside.
2. Mix the mayonnaise and horseradish or wasabi.
3. Using a vegetable peeler, slice the cucumber lengthways into thin ribbons, turning to slice around the core of seeds. Discard the seeds and the first layer of skin on each turn.
4. Mix the dressing ingredients together.
5. Divide the salad greens between 4 plates and drizzle the dressing over. Top each with 2 ribbons of trout or salmon and place a dollop of mayonnaise mixture on the side. Arrange the cucumber ribbons in soft curls over the trout or salmon, sprinkle over the sesame seeds and chives, and top with a feather of dill.

PRAWN AND AVOCADO LETTUCE CUPS
with CRISPY RICE NOODLES

 20 m 5 m 4–6

If you would like the prawns to have a more intense flavour, they can be cooked first and left to marinate in the sauce overnight.

2 Tbsp canola oil
24 prawns, shelled and deveined (thawed and drained if frozen)
2 cloves garlic, peeled and finely chopped
1 tsp fresh peeled and finely chopped fresh ginger
1 red chilli, deseeded and finely chopped
3 Tbsp lemon juice
2 tsp honey
2 ripe avocados

2 tsp lemon juice
2–3 baby gem lettuces, rinsed
2 spring onions, sliced diagonally
a handful of fresh coriander

TOPPING
a small handful of vermicelli dried rice noodles
½ cup oil

1. Heat the oil in a wok or frying pan over a medium heat, then add the prawns, garlic, ginger and chilli. Stir-fry for 2–3 minutes to cook the prawns. As soon as they turn opaque, stir in the 3 Tbsp of lemon juice and honey. Season to taste and pour the prawns and sauce into a dish. Allow to cool. If marinating overnight, cover and refrigerate until needed.
2. Cut the avocados in half lengthways, remove the pip and peel both halves. Slice each half widthways, and drizzle over the 2 tsp lemon juice to prevent browning.
3. Separate the lettuce leaves, dividing the larger leaves between 4–6 side plates. Place a few slices of avocado into each leaf. Scatter over the spring onions, and top with 4–6 prawns each. Pour a little of the sauce over each serving and garnish with the coriander.
4. To prepare the topping, separate the rice noodles and break or cut them into shorter pieces. Heat the oil in a medium saucepan, and to check if it is hot enough, dip in a long noodle to ensure it puffs up immediately. When ready, drop the noodles into the pot, and as soon as they puff (after a few seconds), remove with a slotted spoon onto kitchen paper to drain.
5. To serve, place a small nest of puffed noodles on top of each plate.

TIP: Instead of peeling the avocados first, simply slice them in their skin and then carefully scoop out with a dessertspoon.

ASPARAGUS
with GARLIC MAYO and PARMESAN CRISPS

10 m   5 m   4

This is a wonderful starter for a large party, when asparagus is in season.

⅓ x quantity Parmesan Crisps (page 35)
1 x quantity Garlic Mayonnaise (page 19)
400g fresh asparagus spears

1. Make the Parmesan Crisps and the Garlic Mayonnaise.
2. Break off the woody ends of the asparagus stems and rinse. Cover the base of a wide frying pan with water, no more than 1cm deep, and bring to the boil. Place the asparagus flat in the hot water (the stems shouldn't be submerged in the water, but sitting on top, to prevent them from going soggy). Cover and steam over a medium heat for 3–5 minutes until just tender, depending on thickness of the stems, then remove and drain.
3. To serve, divide the asparagus between 4 warmed plates with a dollop of garlic mayonnaise on the side and a Parmesan Crisp. Alternatively, use Hollandaise Sauce (page 21) in place of Garlic Mayonnaise, as another option.

MUSHROOMS
with MELTED CAPRESE TOPPING

 10 m 20 m 6

This is good as a starter, but it works well as a side dish too

1 Tbsp olive oil
6 large or 12 medium (Portobello) mushrooms, wiped
30g butter
1 clove garlic, peeled and finely chopped
6–12 slices mozzarella cheese
12 baby tomatoes, halved
2 tsp basil pesto

a handful of fresh basil or coriander or flat-leaf parsley for garnishing
2 Tbsp balsamic vinegar
2 Tbsp olive oil
100g fresh rocket
1 small French loaf for serving

1. Preheat the oven to 180°C. Drizzle the oil on a baking tray.
2. Remove the stalks from the mushrooms and arrange them cap-side down on the tray. Dot with a little butter, season to taste and sprinkle over the garlic. Tear the mozzarella slices in half and place on the mushrooms. Top with the tomato halves and a little pesto. Bake for 15–20 minutes, until the mushrooms are fairly tender and the cheese has melted. Garnish as preferred.
3. Mix the balsamic vinegar and oil in a jar, then toss in the rocket leaves. Serve with the mushrooms, along with crusty French bread.

CHEESE AND TOMATO MUSSELS

10 m | 15 m | 4

A quick and easy starter, this dish could also be used as finger food if the mussels are cut from the shell just after steaming, and replaced in the shell for topping and grilling.

420g frozen uncooked mussels in half shells, thawed
20g butter
1 large clove garlic, peeled and finely chopped
½ x 400g can chopped tomatoes
1 cup finely grated Cheddar cheese

1. Preheat the grill.
2. Bring ½ cup water to the boil in a medium saucepan and add the mussels. Cover and steam over a medium heat for 2–3 minutes, until cooked through. Drain and arrange on a large baking sheet in a single layer.
3. Heat the butter in a small saucepan and gently fry the garlic over a low heat for 1 minute, then mash in the tomatoes. Bring to the boil and simmer for 5 minutes until the sauce has slightly reduced. Spoon a little of the mixture over each mussel. Sprinkle the cheese on top and grill for 6 minutes, until the cheese has melted.
4. Serve hot, with a sprinkling of chopped parsley, if desired.

EASY SPINACH SOUFFLÉS

10 m · 20 m · 4

These make excellent light starters, but must be eaten straightaway.

15g butter, melted
200g baby spinach, rinsed
2 eggs, separated
1 small clove garlic, peeled and finely chopped
¼ cup crème fraîche
2 Tbsp crumbled feta

1. Preheat the oven to 180°C. Arrange 4 x 150ml ramekins on a baking tray. Brush the ramekins generously with the melted butter and set aside.
2. Heat ½ cup water in a large pan and wilt the spinach for 2–3 minutes, turning to wilt evenly. Remove and squeeze out the liquid.
3. Blitz the spinach, egg yolks, garlic, crème fraîche and feta in a blender until smooth (about 1 minute). Season to taste.
4. Whip the egg whites until soft peaks form. Carefully fold the spinach mixture into the egg whites, then pour into the ramekins. Bake for 15–18 minutes until set and risen.
5. Serve immediately.

MAIN COURSES

CHICKEN FLORENTINE
with MOZZARELLA

 15 m 20 m 4

Never be tempted to taste chicken dishes before the meat is properly cooked.

4 medium skinless chicken breasts
1 Tbsp oil
30g butter
1 medium onion, peeled and finely chopped
1 large clove garlic, peeled and finely chopped
200g baby spinach, rinsed and patted dry
100g mozzarella cheese, thinly sliced
20 baby tomatoes or vine tomatoes

1. Preheat the oven grill.
2. Trim the chicken breasts, removing any sinew. Cut in half horizontally, then cover in clingfilm on a board, and flatten with a rolling pin to about 5mm thickness. Season with salt and pepper.
3. Heat the oil and half the butter in a large frying pan over a medium heat, and place the chicken pieces in the pan in a single layer. Fry for 3–4 minutes per side, to brown and cook through. Transfer to a wide ovenproof serving dish, arranging them in a single layer, and cover with a tea towel to keep warm.
4. Melt the remaining butter in the same frying pan over a medium heat and add the onion and garlic. Stir-fry for 3 minutes, until softened, scraping in the pan juices. Push to one side of the pan, then add the spinach. Season and wilt the spinach all over for 3 minutes, turning occasionally. Stir in the onion and garlic. Cover the chicken evenly with the spinach mixture. Top with the mozzarella slices and scatter the baby tomatoes over, or place the vine tomatoes across the centre.
5. Grill for 5–7 minutes, until the cheese has melted and browned slightly. Serve immediately with salad or steamed vegetables.

COCONUT CHICKEN CURRY
with TOASTED ALMONDS

 20 m 1 h 4–6

This dish is best made in advance to allow the flavours to develop.

80g flaked almonds
½ cup ground almonds
3 Tbsp oil
1 large onion, peeled and sliced
1 large clove garlic, peeled and finely chopped
2cm piece fresh ginger, peeled and finely chopped
1 chilli, deseeded and finely chopped
2–3 Tbsp mild or medium curry paste or powder
8–12 chicken thighs, skinned and trimmed of excess fat
¾ cup chicken stock
1 x 400ml can coconut cream

1. Toast the flaked almonds in a dry frying pan over a medium heat for 1–2 minutes, shaking the pan to toast the almonds evenly. Transfer from the pan to a small bowl and set aside. Do the same with the ground almonds.
2. Heat half the oil in a large saucepan over a medium heat and fry the onion for 3–4 minutes until soft. Stir in the garlic, ginger, chilli and curry paste or powder, and fry for a further 2 minutes until fragrant.
3. Add the remaining oil and the chicken pieces, coating the chicken in the spices, while frying for a further 5 minutes. Pour in the stock and scrape in the pan crusts, then add half the flaked almonds, all the ground almonds and coconut cream. Bring to the boil, cover and simmer over a low heat for 35 minutes, stirring occasionally to prevent the chicken from sticking to the saucepan. Uncover and cook for a further 10 minutes, to reduce the sauce.
4. Serve with rice, crispy poppadums and little bowls of chopped tomato and onion; chopped cucumber with plain yoghurt and garlic; the remaining toasted almonds; fresh coriander; and fruit chutney.

CHICKEN AND CHORIZO
with TOMATOES

20 m   1 h   4–6

This dish can be prepared in advance and reheated before serving.

2 Tbsp oil
225g spicy chorizo, skinned and thinly sliced
2 red onions, peeled and quartered lengthways.
8–12 medium-to-large chicken thighs,
trimmed of excess fat
1 heaped tsp paprika
1 large clove garlic, peeled and finely chopped
1 tsp dried origanum
1 cup dry white wine
1 cup chicken stock (use only ½ stock cube)
1 x 400g can peeled whole tomatoes in juice

1. Heat the oil in a large saucepan over a medium heat.
2. Fry the chorizo and onions for 7–8 minutes, turning occasionally to soften the onions and release the chorizo oils. Remove with a slotted spoon, and set aside, leaving the red-tinged oil in the pan.
3. Add the chicken pieces to the pan. Sprinkle the paprika, garlic and origanum over, season lightly, and turn the heat up a little. Brown the chicken on both sides, about 4 minutes per side.
4. Pour in the wine and scrape gently around the pan to deglaze. Stir in the chorizo, onions, stock and tomatoes, mashing the tomatoes in with a fork. Reduce the heat to low and simmer, uncovered, for 45 minutes, stirring occasionally.
5. Garnish as desired then serve with baby potatoes or rice, and vegetables.

CHICKEN
in BACON, MUSHROOM and WHITE WINE SAUCE

15 m   55 m   4–6

3 Tbsp oil
150g diced bacon
1 medium red onion, peeled and thinly sliced
2 cloves garlic, peeled and finely chopped
250g button mushrooms, wiped and sliced
8–12 medium chicken thighs, skinned and
trimmed of excess fat
1 tsp origanum
1 sprig fresh thyme or ½ tsp dried thyme
1½ cups dry white wine
½ cup chicken stock
½ cup crème fraîche (optional)

1. Heat the oil in a large saucepan over medium heat and fry the bacon and onion for 5–6 minutes, stirring occasionally, until the bacon is browned and the onion is soft. Add the garlic and mushrooms, and cook for a further 4 minutes. Remove from the pan with a slotted spoon and set aside.

2. Using the same pan, add the chicken pieces, turning to cover them in the pan juices. Sprinkle over the herbs and pour in the wine, scraping in the browned pan juices for extra flavour. Stir in the mushroom mixture and add the stock. Bring to the boil, cover and reduce the heat to low. Simmer for 30 minutes, then uncover. If using the crème fraîche, scoop out 3 or 4 spoons of the sauce from the pan and whisk it into the crème fraîche, then stir it into the pan. Either way, cook uncovered for another 10 minutes, until the sauce has slightly reduced and the chicken cooked through. Season to taste and garnish as desired.

3. Serve with baby potatoes or noodles and steamed vegetables.

CHICKEN
in BEST CURRY MAYO

20 m   15 m   4–6

This is a popular version of Coronation Chicken, which never fails to please.
Make a day or so in advance for best results, and serve cold for summer lunch parties with
a crunchy salad and pita breads or crispy poppadums.

80g flaked almonds
1kg cooked whole chicken (± 500g boneless meat)
1 Tbsp oil
1 small onion, finely chopped
½–1 Tbsp curry paste or powder
1 tsp tomato purée
2 Tbsp lemon juice
2 Tbsp fruit chutney
¾ cup chicken stock
1 cup mayonnaise
½ cup cream

1. Toast the almonds in a dry frying pan over a medium heat for 3–4 minutes, shaking the pan to toast evenly. Transfer from the pan to a small bowl and set aside.
2. Tear the chicken off the bone into roughly finger-size pieces.
3. Heat the oil in a frying pan over a medium heat and fry the onion for 4 minutes until soft. Stir in the curry paste or powder and cook for 2 minutes until fragrant, then stir in the tomato purée, lemon juice, chutney and stock. Continue stirring until it comes to the boil, then reduce the heat and simmer for 5 minutes. Set aside to cool. Stir in the mayonnaise and cream, season to taste and then add the chicken, and half the almonds. Mix well, cover and chill until needed. (It will keep for up to 3 days in the fridge.)
4. When ready to serve, transfer to a platter and scatter over the remaining toasted almonds.

ORIENTAL-STYLE
CHICKEN SALAD

30 m · 2 m · 4–6

This is perfect for lunch parties, served cold with the suggested salad, although any other ready mixed salad (allow about 120g per person) could be used.

1 Tbsp sesame seeds
1kg cooked chicken (± 500g boneless meat)
2 Tbsp soy sauce
2 Tbsp honey
2 Tbsp fresh lime juice
½ tsp sesame oil
1 small red chilli, deseeded
and finely chopped
¾ cup mayonnaise
4 spring onions, trimmed and sliced

SALAD
2 large carrots (±120g), peeled
1 baby red cabbage (±120g), finely shredded
2 sticks celery (±120g), cut into matchsticks
2 baby gem lettuces (±120g), leaves separated
2 ripe avocados
1 Tbsp fresh lime juice
100g sugar snap peas, some shelled
a handful of fresh coriander

SALAD DRESSING
3 Tbsp honey
3 Tbsp fresh lime juice
a few drops of sesame oil
2 Tbsp canola oil

1. Toast the sesame seeds in a dry frying pan over a medium heat for 2 minutes, until fragrant and turning golden. Transfer from the pan to a small bowl to cool.
2. Tear the chicken off the bone into chunky, bite-size pieces, and put into a large bowl. To make a dressing for the chicken, whisk together the soy sauce, honey, lime juice, sesame oil, chilli and mayonnaise. Stir in the spring onions and pour over the chicken. Mix well to combine.
3. For the salad, slice the carrots lengthways into ribbons, using a vegetable peeler. Mix with the cabbage, celery and lettuces in a large bowl.
4. Whisk the salad dressing ingredients together, and toss into the salad. Place the salad on a large serving platter, leaving a space in the centre for the chicken. Peel and slice the avocados, and squeeze over the lime juice. Dot the avocado and sugar snap peas over the salad. Spoon the chicken mixture into the centre and scatter the sesame seeds and coriander leaves over the top.

SLOW-COOKED DUCK LEGS
in ORANGE

 10 m 3 h 4

4–6 duck legs with thighs attached
½ tsp salt
1 tsp Thai 7 spice
1 Tbsp oil
juice of 2 medium oranges (±¾ cup)
1 large clove garlic, peeled and finely chopped
1 small piece fresh ginger, peeled and finely chopped
1½ cups chicken stock

1. Pat the duck skin dry with kitchen paper and pierce all over with a knife point. Rub with the salt and Thai 7 spice.
2. Drizzle the oil into a wide-based saucepan and place the legs skin-side down in a single layer. Cook over a medium heat for 15 minutes, reducing the heat for a further 5 minutes, to render the fat and brown the skin. Lift the duck occasionally to prevent it sticking to the pan. Turn the legs over and cook slowly over a low heat, for a further 40 minutes in the fat, then pour or ladle most of the fat into a large frying pan, and set aside.
3. Pour the orange juice into the saucepan with the duck and scrape in the crusty pan juices, then add the garlic, ginger and stock. Bring to the boil, cover and simmer slowly over low heat for a further 1¾ hours, until the legs are tender. Check the liquid level occasionally and add a little water if needed, stirring in the pan juices as before. The sauce will be deliciously reduced.
4. Heat the reserved fat in the frying pan over a medium heat and place the duck skin-side down in the fat. Fry for 2–3 minutes to crisp the skin.
5. Serve immediately with the sauce spooned over and a side of mashed potato and steamed vegetables.

SEARED DUCK BREAST
with REDCURRANT SAUCE

 5 m 15 m 5–10 m  4

The combination of succulent duck with an intense fruity sauce is a real treat.

4 duck breasts
salt for rubbing
1 Tbsp white wine vinegar

3 Tbsp redcurrant jelly
2 tsp soy sauce

1. Pat the duck skin dry with kitchen paper, then rub salt into the skin.
2. Place the duck skin-side down in a single layer in a large, dry frying pan. Place over a medium heat and leave to render the fat and crisp the skin for 7–9 minutes. Reduce the heat and turn the duck over. Cook for a further 2–3 minutes, until cooked but still pink in the middle. Transfer from the pan to a dish, cover and set aside to rest.
3. Make the sauce by first pouring off most of the fat in the pan, but keeping the meaty pan juices. Add the vinegar, redcurrant jelly and soy sauce, and stir well, over a medium to low heat, for 2–3 minutes, to dissolve the jelly and slightly reduce the sauce. Pour into a small serving bowl.
4. To serve, slice the duck widthways at an angle and drizzle with a little of the sauce. Serve with crispy potatoes and fresh salad or steamed vegetables.

BEST HOME-MADE BURGERS

20 m   10 m + topping   5 m   6

These burgers are succulent and delicious with or without a bun. Simple, patted into shape and cooked until just done, they are winners in their own right, but if you dress them up with a tasty topping they are dinner-party-worthy with minimal effort.

900g mostly lean beef mince (a little fat needed)
1 Tbsp Dijon mustard
1 Tbsp olive oil
6 buns, halved (optional)

1. Season the mince and lightly (for a more succulent burger) fold in the mustard. Divide the mince into 6 equal portions. Shape into rounded patties, without squashing them too much. Press a thumbprint in the middle of the top of each patty (to prevent bulging when cooking) and sprinkle with a little more salt and pepper.

2. Heat the oil in a large frying pan over a medium heat, then add the burgers and fry for 3–4 minutes per side, for a browned crust and pink centre. Don't squash down on the burgers during cooking. Fry for an extra 2 minutes for a well-done finish; any longer will dry the burgers out. Cover to keep warm and set aside to rest for 4–5 minutes. Meanwhile, make the desired sauce or topping.

TOPPINGS

Prepare one or any combination of the following toppings or sauces:

Caramelised onions: Page 24.

Cheese: Top each burger with a slice of cheese. Cover with a lid to keep warm and rest for 5 minutes, during which time the cheese will melt slightly.

Blue cheese sauce: Heat ¾ cup cream over a medium heat and crumble 100g blue cheese into the cream. Whisk to melt the cheese, then simmer gently for 4–5 minutes to thicken.

Mustard sauce: Combine ½ cup cream, ½ cup strong chicken stock and 2 tsp wholegrain mustard in a saucepan. Bring to the boil and simmer over a low heat for 10 minutes until reduced and creamy.

Mushroom sauce: Gently fry 1 small sliced onion and 1 small chopped clove garlic in 1 Tbsp oil for 3 minutes. Stir in 250g sliced mushrooms with 15g butter and then fry for 3 minutes. Stir in ¾ cup cream and 1 Tbsp soy sauce. Simmer over a medium to low heat for 6–7 minutes until thickened.

Poached egg and fried bacon: Fry 1–2 rashers bacon per person, in 1 Tbsp oil over a medium heat, until browned. Bring a saucepan of water to the boil, reduce the heat until the bubbles stop, and carefully crack in 1 egg per person. Turn up the heat slightly and poach for 3 minutes per egg. Remove with a slotted spoon, onto a plate, and dab any excess water on the plate with kitchen paper. Repeat for the remaining eggs. Top each burger with the bacon and egg.

MEXICAN-STYLE BEEF TORTILLAS
with GUACAMOLE, CHEESE and SOUR CREAM

15 m 45 m 4

Instead of using tortillas, try making your own flat breads (page 134).

1 tsp coriander seeds
1 tsp cumin seeds or ½ tsp ground cumin
1 Tbsp oil
1 large onion, peeled and finely chopped
2 cloves garlic, peeled and finely chopped
1½ Tbsp paprika
1 red chilli, deseeded and finely chopped
1kg beef mince
1 x 400g can tomatoes
2 Tbsp tomato paste
1 tsp Worcestershire sauce

1 cup beef stock
8–12 wraps or tortillas
1 cup grated Cheddar cheese
1 cup sour cream

GUACAMOLE
2 avocados
2 tsp fresh lime juice
1 rounded tsp mayonnaise
a few drops of Tabasco
1 Tbsp chopped fresh coriander

1. Crush the coriander and cumin seeds in a cup with a pestle or handle of a wooden spoon.
2. Heat the oil in a large saucepan over a medium heat and fry the onion for 3–4 minutes, until softened. Add the garlic, ground coriander and cumin, paprika and chilli, then fry for 1–2 minutes, until fragrant. Stir in the mince, chopping through it with a spoon, until it's brown and crumbly. Mash in the tomatoes, then add the tomato paste, Worcestershire sauce and stock. Season and mix well. Bring to the boil, turn the heat to low, cover and simmer for 30 minutes, stirring occasionally.
3. Meanwhile, make the guacamole by halving the avocados lengthways, remove the pip and scoop out the flesh into a bowl. Mash with a fork and mix in the remaining ingredients until smooth or chunky, as you prefer.
4. Spoon the mince into a warm serving dish, and serve with the tortillas on a plate and the guacamole, cheese and sour cream in separate dishes. Everyone can help themselves.

BEEF STEAKS
with PEPPER SAUCE

5 m · 20 m · 5–10 m · 4

2 tsp oil
4 x 200–250g beef steaks (2–2.5cm thick)
10g butter
1 small onion, peeled and finely chopped
1 cup cream
2 tsp ground black pepper
1 Tbsp Dijon mustard
1 Tbsp soy sauce

1. Heat the oil in a frying pan over a medium to high heat, and sear the steaks, 3–4 minutes on each side, for medium-rare, then remove from the pan onto a wooden board and cover with foil to rest and keep warm.
2. Melt the butter in the steak pan, add the onion and scrape in the meat juices for extra flavour. Fry over a medium heat for 3 minutes, stirring occasionally, until softened.
3. Add the cream, pepper, mustard and soy sauce, and slowly bring to the boil while stirring. Reduce the heat to very low, and simmer gently for 5 minutes until reduced and thickened slightly.
4. Pour the sauce over the steaks and serve immediately, with vegetables or salad.

STEAKS
with MUSHROOMS and RED WINE REDUCTION

10 m   25 m   5–10 m   4

The sauce in this recipe is very quick and simple to make and will add a touch of luxury to the steak.

2 tsp oil
4 x 200–250g beef steaks (2–2½cm thick)
30g butter, plus 15g extra
1 small red onion, peeled and thinly sliced
100g Portabello mushrooms, wiped and sliced
1 small sprig of fresh thyme or ¼ tsp dried thyme
1 cup red wine
1 cup beef stock

1. Heat the oil in a frying pan over a medium to high heat, then sear the steaks, 3–4 minutes on each side for medium-rare. Transfer them to a wooden board and cover with foil to rest and keep warm.
2. Melt the 30g of butter in the same pan, and add the onion. Cook over medium heat for 3 minutes until softened, then add the mushrooms and thyme. Cook for a further 2 minutes, stirring occasionally.
3. Pour in the wine, stirring in the pan juices. Cook over a medium heat for 3 minutes, until reduced. Add the beef stock and cook for 5–7 minutes, until reduced by almost half. Remove from the heat and mix in the extra butter.
4. Spoon the sauce over the steaks and serve with vegetables or salad

STIR-FRY BEEF
in HOISIN SAUCE

20 m   10 m   4

This is a quick meal to prepare in a wok, ready to serve with instant egg noodles.

600g beef steak, thinly sliced
2 Tbsp soy sauce
300g instant egg noodles
2 tsp sesame oil
2 Tbsp canola oil
250g mushrooms, wiped and thinly sliced
4 spring onions, trimmed, sliced lengthways and cut into 3 or 4 pieces
1 small red chilli, deseeded and finely chopped
1 large clove garlic, peeled and finely chopped or grated
1 x 230g can bamboo shoots, rinsed and drained
8–12 baby corn, sliced in half lengthways
100g sugar snap peas, sliced in half lengthways
2 Tbsp hoisin sauce
¼ cup beef stock

1. Mix the beef slices with the soy sauce.
2. Cook the noodles according to the packet instructions, drain and toss in the sesame oil.
3. Heat the canola oil in a wok or large frying pan over a medium to high heat and add the beef. Stir-fry for 2–3 minutes, to brown all over. Reduce the heat to medium, then add the mushrooms, spring onions, chilli and garlic. Stir-fry for 2–3 minutes. Add the bamboo shoots, baby corn and sugar snap peas. Stir-fry for a further 2 minutes, until heated through.
4. Mix the hoisin sauce with the stock and pour into the wok. Stir for 1 minute before adding the cooked noodles and serving.

BEEF PAPRIKASH

10 m   3 h   4–6

This is a lovely warming stew that can be made in advance.
It's ideal for informal entertaining for friends and family.

3 Tbsp oil
2 medium onions, peeled and sliced
3 Tbsp paprika
1kg stewing beef, cut into cubes
2 large cloves garlic, peeled and
finely chopped
1 rounded tsp dried origanum
2 Tbsp red wine vinegar
2 Tbsp tomato paste
½ red pepper, deseeded and chopped
1 cup sour cream for serving

1. Heat the oil in a large saucepan over a medium heat, and fry the onions for 4 minutes, until softened. Add the paprika, beef and half a cup of water. Bring to the boil and simmer over a medium to high heat for 10–15 minutes, until the liquid has reduced to almost nothing. Stir occasionally.
2. Mix in the garlic, origanum, vinegar, tomato paste and red pepper. Stir in 2–3 cups water. Season to taste, cover and bring to the boil. Simmer over a low heat for 2½ hours, until tender, occasionally stirring and checking the liquid level. Add a little more water if necessary.
3. Serve with noodles and a dollop of sour cream. Garnish as desired.

OSTRICH STEAKS
in PORT

5 m | 15 m | 5–10 m | 4

Ostrich is a tasty, lean meat with a gamey flavour. Fortunately, it's widely available in supermarkets, and often very reasonable in price.

4 x 150–200g ostrich steaks | ½ cup Port (or Cape Ruby or Cape Tawny)
1 Tbsp oil | ½ cup beef stock
30g butter | 1 sprig of fresh thyme

1. Season the ostrich steaks on both sides.
2. Heat the oil and half the butter in a large frying pan over a medium to high heat. Sear the ostrich steaks, 3 minutes per side, then pour in the port. Cook for a further minute on each side, for medium-rare, depending on the thickness of the steaks. Leaving the juices in the pan, transfer the meat to a warm plate and cover with foil to rest and keep warm.
3. Pour the stock into the pan and scrape in the meaty juices. Add the thyme and simmer for 2–3 minutes, stirring until the sauce has slightly reduced. Remove from the heat, discard the thyme and stir in the remaining butter to enrich the sauce.
4. Spoon the sauce over the steaks and serve immediately with fresh vegetables, or vegetable purée, on the side.

OSTRICH STEAKS
in REDCURRANT and ROSEMARY SAUCE

5 m   15 m   5–10 m   4

4 x 150–200g ostrich steaks	1 cup beef stock
1 Tbsp oil	3 Tbsp redcurrant jelly
15g butter	1 tsp balsamic vinegar
	1 small sprig of fresh rosemary

1. Season the ostrich steaks on both sides. Heat the oil and butter in a large frying pan over a medium to high heat, then sear the steaks, 3–4 minutes per side for medium-rare, depending on the thickness of the steaks. Transfer to a warm plate and cover with foil to rest and keep warm.
2. Add the stock to the pan, scraping in the meaty juices, and mix in the redcurrant jelly, vinegar and rosemary. Boil over a medium to high heat for 5 minutes until reduced and syrupy. Discard the rosemary.
3. Spoon the sauce over the steaks and serve immediately, with fresh vegetables.

PORK FILLET
in TARRAGON CREAM

600–650g pork fillet, silver skin removed
1 Tbsp soy sauce
1 clove garlic, peeled and finely chopped
½ cup chicken stock
½ cup crème fraîche
2 tsp Dijon mustard
2 tsp dried tarragon
1 Tbsp olive oil

1. Thinly slice the pork and mix with the soy sauce and garlic.
2. Whisk the stock and crème fraîche until smooth, then stir in the mustard and tarragon.
3. Heat the oil in a large frying pan over medium heat. Fry the pork slices with the soy sauce and garlic for 2–3 minutes on each side, to brown all over. Pour in the crème fraîche sauce, and mix into the pork, scraping in the pan juices. Bring to the boil, stirring, and simmer gently over a low heat to 5–6 minutes, until the sauce has slightly reduced and the pork cooked through. Season to taste.
4. Garnish as desired. Serve with rice or noodles and fresh vegetables.

PORK FILLET
in BACON with APPLE and GINGER CREAM

This works equally well with smoked or unsmoked pork.

200g streaky bacon
600–650g (smoked or plain) pork fillet, silver skin removed
2 Tbsp oil
15g butter
1 shallot or small onion, peeled and finely chopped
1 apple, peeled, cored and finely chopped
1 tsp finely chopped fresh ginger or ½ tsp ground ginger
2 tsp white wine vinegar
½ cup chicken stock
½ cup cream

1. Preheat the oven to 200°C.
2. Arrange the bacon lengthways and just overlapping on a board. Place the pork fillet along one edge of the bacon ends, then roll the pork up tightly in the bacon. (If 2 fillets are used, use half the bacon, spaced apart for each fillet.)
3. Heat half the oil in a large frying pan over a medium to high heat and brown the wrapped pork all over, for 2 minutes per side. Set the pan with juices aside, to make the sauce.
4. Lightly drizzle a baking tray with the remaining oil. Place the wrapped pork sealed-side down in the baking tray and roast in the oven for 10 minutes, until the pork is just cooked through, with a pink blush in the middle. Remove from the oven, cover loosely with foil and set aside to rest.
5. Meanwhile, make the sauce by melting the butter in the frying pan, then adding the shallot or onion, apple and ginger. Cover and sweat over a medium heat for 5 minutes, stirring occasionally. Add the vinegar and cook, uncovered, for 2 minutes. Pour in the stock and simmer for 3 minutes, until reduced. Stir in the cream and simmer over a low heat for 6–8 minutes, until the sauce thickens. Blitz the sauce in a blender until smooth, or mash by hand. Season to taste.
6. Serve the pork sliced with the sauce poured over, with mashed potato mixed with a tablespoon of wholegrain mustard, and fresh vegetables.

PORK STEAKS
with CRISPY SAGE and WINE REDUCTION

5 m | 25 m | 4

If you prefer, you could use pork chops instead of steaks.

1 Tbsp oil
30g butter
4 x 200g lean pork steaks
a handful of fresh sage
1 shallot or small onion, peeled and
finely chopped
½ cup white wine
1 cup chicken stock

1. Heat the oil and half the butter in a large frying pan over a medium heat.
2. Season the pork and add to the pan. Fry for 3–4 minutes on each side, until browned and cooked through, then transfer the meat to a warm dish, cover with foil and set aside.
3. Add most of the sage leaves to the pan and cook for 2–3 minutes, turning to crisp on both sides. Remove and set aside for garnish. Add the remaining leaves to the pan with the shallot or onion and gently fry for 4 minutes, until the shallot or onion is soft. Pour in the wine, stirring in the pan juices, and allow to bubble over a medium to high heat for 2 minutes, until slightly reduced. Add the stock and reduce by almost half (5–7 minutes). Remove from the heat and stir in the remaining butter.
4. Serve the pork with the sauce spooned over, topped with the crispy sage leaves, and fresh steamed vegetables on the side.

CRISPY PORK BELLY

10 m   4 h–overnight   65 m   4

To ensure the best flavour, marinate the pork belly for at least 4 hours, or preferably overnight.

2 tsp salt
1kg boneless pork belly
pepper to taste
1 whole bulb garlic
2 cups chicken stock

MARINADE
2 Tbsp soy sauce
2 Tbsp white wine vinegar
1 Tbsp honey

1. Rub half the salt over the pork skin.
2. To make the marinade, mix the soy sauce, vinegar and honey in a container big enough to accommodate the pork belly. Place the pork in the mixture flesh-side down and marinate for a minimum of 4 hours.
3. Preheat the oven to 180°C.
4. Remove the pork from the marinade, reserving the marinade for the sauce. Wipe the salt off the skin (which should be full of drawn-out moisture by this stage) and pat dry with kitchen paper. Rub the remaining salt and some pepper into the skin.
5. Cut the garlic bulb in half horizontally, and place cut-side up in a roasting tin, with the pork on top. Roast for 45 minutes, then remove from the oven. Increase the oven temperature to 220°C.
6. Remove the garlic and return the pork to the roasting tin and roast for a further 20 minutes in the hot oven, until the skin is golden and crispy. Grill for a final 2 minutes, if necessary.
7. Meanwhile, make the sauce by pouring the reserved marinade into a saucepan, add the chicken stock and 2 or 3 cloves of the roasted garlic squeezed out of the skin, and bring to the boil. Cook over a medium heat for 15–20 minutes, until it has reduced by half.
8. Serve the pork sliced into fingers with the sauce, and hot buttered baby cabbage (sliced and steamed in a little water and butter for 3 minutes).

ROAST GAMMON
in CIDER

This dish is ideal for making over the weekend for lunch parties. Even without the glaze it's delicious, but if you prefer a sweet or savoury topping, it's simple to add the glaze before the last half-hour of cooking.

1 Tbsp oil
2 carrots, peeled and chopped
1 large onion, peeled and sliced
2 sticks celery, sliced
6 black peppercorns
2 dried bay leaves

1.5kg boneless gammon, skin and fat on
2 x 330ml bottles cider

GLAZE (OPTIONAL)
1 tsp runny honey
1 rounded tsp Dijon mustard

1. Preheat the oven to 160°C. Drizzle the oil in a deep roasting tin.
2. Arrange a bed of carrots, onion, celery, peppercorns and bay leaves in the roasting tin. Place the gammon on top. Pour over the cider, and cover the tin with a lid or foil. Roast for 1½ hours (30 minutes per 500g). Remove from the oven, and increase the heat to 200°C. Take out the gammon and pour most of the cooking liquid, along with the onions and vegetables, into a container. This could later be used to make a delicious soup.
3. Place the gammon back into the roasting tin and peel off the skin, but do not remove the layer of fat just beneath the skin. Using the tip of a sharp knife, score a diamond pattern lightly into the fat layer. To glaze the roast (if using), mix the honey and mustard together (for a sweet glaze), or the mustard on its own (for a savoury topping), and brush it all over the scored fat.
4. Return the gammon to the oven to roast, uncovered, for a further 30 minutes, until the top is golden and sizzling. At the same time, put the skin on a separate oven tray and roast for 20–30 minutes to make crispy crackling. Remove both dishes from the oven and allow the gammon to rest for 20 minutes, if serving hot, or allow to cool until needed. Break the crackling into shards.
5. Serve the gammon thinly sliced with a shard of crackling and salads of your choice.

PULLED PORK
in BARBECUE SAUCE

20 m   3¾–6 h   6–8

For best results this recipe needs 3½–4 hours in the oven or 5–6 hours on 'high' in a slow cooker. It is an ideal party dish, and can be served in wraps, pita breads or buns with a Red Coleslaw Salad (page 137), or it can be presented on a large platter surrounded by coleslaw.

1 tsp salt and some freshly ground black pepper
1 Tbsp prepared mustard
1 tsp ground cumin
1 Tbsp smoked paprika
1 tsp ground ginger
1 Tbsp oil plus extra for drizzling
1.5kg boneless pork neck
1 large red onion, peeled and sliced
2 cloves garlic, peeled and sliced
1 large carrot, peeled and sliced
2 bay leaves
1 litre chicken stock

BARBECUE SAUCE

1 Tbsp Worcestershire sauce
2 Tbsp tomato sauce
1 Tbsp red wine vinegar
1 tsp smoked paprika
2 Tbsp brown sugar

1. Preheat the oven to 160°C or set a slow cooker to 'high'.
2. Combine the salt, pepper, mustard, cumin, paprika, ginger and 1 Tbsp oil in a bowl, to make a thick paste. Rub the mixture all over the pork.
3. Drizzle some oil in a large ovenproof saucepan or deep roasting tin or slow cooker, then cover the base with the onion, garlic, carrot and bay leaves. Place the pork on top and pour in the stock. Cover with a lid or foil, and roast in the oven for 3½–4 hours or in a slow cooker for 5–6 hours. When the meat is tender enough to pick out a piece easily with a fork, transfer it to a rimmed tray to cool slightly, and strain the liquid from the meat into a medium saucepan, for the sauce (about 2 cups). Shred the meat with your fingers into good bite-size chunks, removing any fat and sinew, and set aside.
4. To make the barbecue sauce, stir all the ingredients into the saucepan with the meat liquid and bring to the boil. Simmer over a low heat, stirring occasionally, for 8–10 minutes, then mix in the pulled meat. This can be stored in a sealed container in the fridge for a few days, or frozen and then reheated when ready to serve with a fresh coleslaw salad. And if you would like to serve it as a snack, it will stretch to 16 people.

PORK SALAD
with FRUIT AND NUTS

20 m · 25 m · 5–10 m · 4–6

This variation on a Waldorf salad with succulent pork fillet is perfect for a lunch party, served either warm or cold.

2 Tbsp oil
½ cup pecan nuts, roughly broken
6 rashers bacon, diced
800g pork fillet, silver skin removed
2 baby gem lettuces, rinsed and leaves separated
2 crisp sweet apples, washed
1 Tbsp lemon juice
2 sticks celery, rinsed and cut into matchsticks
1 small red onion, peeled and thinly sliced
1 cup seedless red grapes, halved

DRESSING
½ cup mayonnaise
1 tsp Dijon mustard
1 Tbsp lemon juice
1 Tbsp honey

1. Preheat the oven to 200°C. Drizzle 1 Tbsp of the oil over a baking tray.
2. Dry-fry the pecan nuts in a frying pan for 3–4 minutes, shaking the pan to toast evenly. Remove and set aside.
3. Heat the remaining oil in a large frying pan over a medium heat and fry the bacon for 3 minutes, until brown. Remove from the pan and set aside.
4. Add the pork fillet to the pan, turn up the heat to medium to high and brown evenly all over, 2 minutes per side. Keep the pan and cooking juices aside, and transfer the pork to the prepared baking tray. Roast for 8–10 minutes, then remove and cover loosely with foil, to rest.
5. Meanwhile, whisk together the ingredients for the dressing, then pour into the cooled, reserved frying pan, stirring in the pan juices.
6. To assemble the salad, arrange the lettuce leaves on a large serving platter. Quarter and core the apples, then slice them thinly. Pour the lemon juice over the apple slices to prevent them from browning. Either scatter the apple slices, celery, onion and grapes over the lettuce, or place them alongside. Sprinkle the nuts and bacon bits over. Slice the pork and arrange on top of the salad. Spoon most of the dressing over the meat and drizzle a little over the rest of the salad, or serve it on the side.
7. Serve immediately.

LAMB STEAKS
with MINT PESTO

 10 m 10 m 1 c pesto  5 m 4

If you prefer, you could use lamb loin or rib chops (2 or 3 per person) instead of steaks. To measure the 'packed' herbs, simply press down the leaves in the cup (stalks removed) and fill to the quantity indicated.

4 x 150–200g lamb steaks (or 8–12 loin or rib chops)
1 Tbsp oil

MINT PESTO
¼ cup roasted salted cashew nuts
1 medium clove garlic, peeled and roughly chopped
1½ Tbsp lemon juice
1½ cups packed fresh mint, rinsed and patted dry
½ cup packed fresh coriander, rinsed and patted dry
2 Tbsp freshly grated Parmesan
½ tsp salt
freshly ground black pepper
½ cup canola oil

1. Preheat the grill.
2. First make the pesto by blitzing all the ingredients together in a food processor. Check the seasoning.
3. Season the lamb steaks (or chops) on both sides, drizzle with the oil and place on a rack on a grill tray. Cook under a hot grill on both sides until browned, but still pink in the centre (3–4 minutes on each side). Remove, cover loosely with foil and rest for 5 minutes.
4. Serve with a spoon of the pesto on each steak, and steamed vegetables on the side.

LAMB CHOPS
with ANCHOVY CAPER SAUCE and VINE TOMATOES

5 m   15 m   4

The anchovies add a rich depth to the flavour of this dish.

8–12 lamb chops
12 vine or cherry tomatoes
50g butter
1 large clove garlic, peeled and
finely chopped
4 anchovies, finely chopped
2 Tbsp baby capers
1 Tbsp lemon juice
1 Tbsp finely chopped fresh parsley
for garnishing

1. Preheat the grill.
2. Season the chops all over. Place them and the tomatoes on a rack in a grill pan, and grill for 4–6 minutes each side until the lamb is browned on the outside and pink in the middle. Remove and keep warm.
3. For the sauce, melt the butter in a small pan over a medium to low heat, and fry the garlic and anchovies for 2–3 minutes until fragrant. Stir in the capers and lemon juice.
4. Spoon the sauce over the chops and sprinkle with the parsley. Serve with the grilled tomatoes and some steamed green beans or courgettes (baby marrows) on the side.

SPICED LAMB
with COUSCOUS

This is an easy, home-made version of harissa paste, spread over lamb steaks (or chops if you prefer) with a simple side dish of couscous.

4 x 200g lamb steaks	HARISSA PASTE
½ cup plain yoghurt	2 tsp cumin seeds
a handful of fresh coriander, torn	2 tsp coriander seeds
	1 small red chilli, deseeded and finely chopped
	1 large clove garlic, peeled and finely chopped
COUSCOUS	1 tsp smoked paprika
1 cup uncooked couscous	4 Tbsp oil
2 Tbsp oil	4 tsp tomato paste
1 Tbsp lemon juice	
1 tsp ground cumin	

1. First prepare the couscous by placing it in a medium-sized bowl and pouring over just enough boiling water to cover. Cover with clingfilm and leave to stand for 10 minutes, until the water has been fully absorbed. Remove the clingfilm and fluff up the couscous with a fork. Stir in the oil, lemon juice and ground cumin, and season to taste.
2. Meanwhile, prepare the harissa by toasting the cumin and coriander seeds in a dry frying pan over a medium heat for 2 minutes, until fragrant. Transfer them into a bowl or mortar, and crush with the chilli, garlic, paprika, oil, tomato paste and a little salt and pepper, to form a rough paste.
3. Preheat the grill.
4. Spread the harissa paste over both sides of the lamb steaks and place them on a rack in a grill pan. Grill for 4–6 minutes per side, until browned and still pink in the middle.
5. To serve, place a couple of spoons of couscous on each plate and top with a lamb steak. Spoon a dollop of yoghurt over the lamb and garnish with the fresh coriander. If you like, you could even swirl a little of the harissa paste through the yoghurt and serve it on the side

SLOW-COOKED LAMB

10 m   4–6¼ h   4–6

This is one of my family's favourites. The succulent, fall-off-the-bone lamb in a tasty rich sauce can be made in advance and may be cooked either in a slow cooker or in the oven. If using lamb shoulder, it's best cooked on the bone in the oven.

1 Tbsp paprika	1 x 400g can whole peeled Italian tomatoes in
1.5–2kg lamb shoulder or 4–6 shanks	tomato juice
1–2 Tbsp oil	2 cups red wine
1 large onion, peeled and sliced	1 litre strong beef stock
1 large clove garlic, peeled and finely chopped	1 sprig of fresh rosemary

IF ROASTING IN THE OVEN:

1. Preheat the oven to 180°C. Rub salt, pepper and the paprika over the lamb. Drizzle 1 Tbsp of the oil in a large, deep ovenproof roasting tin, and place the lamb in the tin. Brown in the oven for 5 minutes on each side.
2. Heat 1 Tbsp oil in a large saucepan over a medium heat and fry the onion for 3 minutes to soften, then add the garlic and cook for another minute. Mash in the tomatoes and pour in the wine and stock. Pour the sauce over the lamb and add the rosemary.
3. Cover the roasting tin securely with foil. To avoid any spills, place a rimmed baking tray underneath, to catch any overflow. Turn the oven down to 170°C, and roast the lamb for 3½–4 hours, until the meat is soft enough to pick out a piece easily with a fork.

IF USING A SLOW COOKER:

1. Switch the cooker on high. Rub salt, pepper and the paprika over the lamb and place the shanks in the cooker.
2. Heat 1 Tbsp of oil in a large saucepan over a medium heat and fry the onion for 3 minutes to soften, then add the garlic and cook for another minute. Mash in the tomatoes and pour in the wine and stock. Pour the sauce over the lamb and add the rosemary.
3. Place the lid on the slow cooker and cook for 6 hours until the meat is soft enough to pick out a piece easily with a fork.

WHICHEVER COOKING METHOD IS USED:

4. When the meat is ready, decant the sauce into a large saucepan. Cover the meat with foil to keep it warm.
5. To make the gravy, pour off the excess fat from the sauce, discard the rosemary and allow to reduce over a fairly high heat for 10–15 minutes. If using lamb shoulder, remove the meat from the bone, discarding any fat and sinew. Lamb shanks are best kept on the bone. Serve with the gravy and vegetables of your choice.

117

GRILLED FISH
with SALSA VERDE on SPINACH

15 m   15 m   4

Salsa verde is a green sauce made mainly with herbs. Serving it with fish on a bed of wilted spinach will not only be tasty, but will also create a beautiful palette of greens against the whiteness of the fish.

SALSA VERDE	SPINACH
2 Tbsp flaked almonds	15g butter
2 Tbsp olive oil	200g baby spinach, rinsed
2 Tbsp freshly squeezed lemon juice	
1 small clove garlic, peeled and finely chopped	FISH
½ cup chopped fresh flat-leaf parsley	2 Tbsp olive oil
2 Tbsp chopped fresh chives	4 x 150g firm white fish fillets, skin on
2 tsp baby capers	2 tsp lemon juice

1. Preheat the grill. Line a grill pan with foil.
2. To prepare the salsa verde, toast the almonds in a dry frying pan over a medium heat for 2–3 minutes, shaking the pan to toast evenly. Transfer them to a bowl, along with the rest of the sauce ingredients and lightly crush with a pestle or wooden spoon, to bring out the flavours. Set aside.
3. To cook the spinach, melt the butter in a frying pan. Add the spinach and cook for 2 minutes, turning to wilt it evenly. Drain well and keep warm.
4. For the fish, drizzle half the oil over the prepared grill pan. Season the fish and place in the pan skin-side up. Drizzle with the lemon juice and remaining oil, then grill for 6–7 minutes, until the skin is crispy and the fish is turning opaque halfway through. Turn over and grill for a further 3–4 minutes, until just done.
5. Meanwhile, heat the salsa either in a microwave oven or in a small saucepan for 1 minute, to warm through. To serve, divide the spinach evenly between warmed serving plates. Place the cooked fish on top and serve with the warmed sauce spooned over, and lemon wedges on the side if you like.

RICH FISH PIE

10 m   45 m   6

This is ideal for an informal gathering of family or friends, and can be made in advance, to be reheated later. It fits into a 1.2-litre baking dish.

2 medium potatoes, peeled and halved
2 cups milk
300g skinless smoked haddock fillets, thawed if frozen
300g skinless hake fillets, thawed if frozen
½ cup white wine
300g shelled and deveined prawns or shrimps, thawed if frozen
35g butter plus 15g for topping
3½ Tbsp cake flour
35g Cheddar cheese, grated
a pinch of cayenne pepper

1. Preheat the oven to 180°C.
2. Boil the potatoes for 12 minutes, then drain and cool slightly before slicing thinly.
3. Meanwhile, pour the milk into a large pan, and bring almost to the boil. Add the haddock and hake, half cover with a lid, and poach gently over a low heat for 6–8 minutes, until opaque. Transfer the fish to a baking dish, reserving the milk for the sauce. Press lightly on the fish with a fork to flake into large pieces.
4. Heat the wine in a separate saucepan and poach the prawns or shrimps for 2 minutes, then remove them with a slotted spoon and scatter them over the flaked fish. Pour the wine into a small bowl and reserve it for the sauce.
5. To make the sauce, melt the 35g butter in the saucepan, mix in the flour and cook gently for 1 minute over a medium to low heat. Remove the pan from the heat, pour in a little of the poaching milk and whisk until smooth. Gradually stir in the remaining milk and the wine, then return the saucepan to the heat. Keep stirring until the sauce thickens and comes to the boil. Stir in most of the grated cheese until melted, add a pinch of cayenne pepper, then season to taste.
6. Pour the sauce over the fish and prawns, and gently fork through to mix in the sauce. Arrange the potato slices on top in one overlapping layer, dot with the remaining butter and sprinkle over the remaining cheese. Bake for 30 minutes, until bubbling and golden on top. Garnish as desired and serve with baby peas and carrots.

FISH IN NUTTY BUTTER
and GREEN PEPPERCORN SAUCE

 5 m   10 m   4

4 x 150–200g firm white fish steaks	SAUCE
20g butter	50g butter
1 clove garlic, peeled and finely chopped	1 Tbsp lemon juice
4 lemon wedges	1 Tbsp green peppercorns

1. Season the fish. Melt the 20g butter in a large frying pan over a medium heat, then add the garlic and fish. Fry for 3 minutes per side for thicker steaks, or 1–2 minutes per side for thinner fish steaks, until just cooked. Remove and cover to keep warm.
2. For the sauce, melt the butter in a small saucepan over medium heat to foam the butter. When it starts to turn brown and give off a nutty aroma (after about 3 minutes), remove immediately from the heat and swirl in the lemon juice and peppercorns.
3. Serve the fish with the sauce spooned over, with lemon wedges and fresh vegetables.

FISH IN ROMESCO SAUCE

10 m   50 m   4

This dish is based on a Spanish-style red pepper, tomato and almond sauce, that has been spiced up a little.

4 x 150–200g firm white fish fillets
a handful of fresh flat-leaf parsley, chopped

SAUCE
4 tsp oil
1 large red pepper, quartered lengthways, deseeded and pith removed
¼ cup flaked almonds
1 large clove garlic, peeled and roughly chopped
½ red chilli, deseeded and finely chopped
½ tsp smoked paprika
1 x 400g can whole Italian tomatoes in juice
½ cup chicken stock
2 Tbsp red wine vinegar

1. Preheat the grill.
2. To prepare the sauce, drizzle 1 tsp of the oil in a grill pan and place the red pepper skin-side up in the pan. Drizzle another teaspoon of oil over and grill for 15–20 minutes, to brown and blister the pepper skin. Remove from the grill and, when cool enough, peel off the skin from top to bottom with the tip of a knife. Slice the pepper into strips.
3. Preheat the oven to 180°C.
4. Heat a dry frying pan over medium heat, and toast the almonds for 2–3 minutes until golden, shaking the pan to toast evenly. Remove the almonds from the pan and set aside.
5. Add the remaining oil to the frying pan and heat over a medium to low heat. Fry the garlic, chilli and paprika for 1–2 minutes until fragrant. Add the pepper strips, tomatoes, stock and vinegar, and simmer for 7–8 minutes. Remove from the heat and leave to cool slightly. Add the almonds to the mixture and blitz with a stick blender, until just slightly chunky. Season well.
6. Pour the sauce into a baking dish, nestle in the fish and bake for 20 minutes until the fish is just cooked through and the sauce bubbling. Serve with the chopped parsley sprinkled over and fresh salad or vegetables on the side.

BAKED WHOLE FISH
with HOLLANDAISE and THYME SAUCE

 9 m   40 m   4

1 Tbsp oil
1 kg firm white fish
1 lemon, sliced
1 large clove garlic,
unpeeled, lightly squashed
1 sprig of fresh thyme

1 x quantity Hollandaise
Sauce (page 21)*
1 tsp lemon juice*
½ tsp chopped fresh
thyme*

1. Preheat the oven to 180°C.
2. Line a baking tray with baking paper, drizzle with the oil and place the fish on top. Open the fish slightly along the bone down the middle, and tuck in most of the lemon slices (reserving 4 slices for garnish), the garlic and sprig of thyme along the length. Bake for 25–30 minutes, until the flesh is just flaking.
3. *Meanwhile make the Hollandaise sauce (page 21), but add an extra teaspoon of lemon juice to the sauce at the beginning, and mix in the chopped thyme at the end. When the fish is cooked, squeeze the soft garlic clove out of the skin and mix into the sauce.
4. To serve, remove the skin and lift the fish off the bone. Place half a fillet on each plate. Turn the fish over and repeat with the other side. Discard the cooked lemon slices and sprig of thyme. Serve the fish with a fresh lemon slice on top and the sauce on the side. This dish goes well with rice and a fresh salad on the side.

SEARED TUNA
in SESAME SEEDS
with PEANUT SAUCE

10 m · 4 m · 2–3 m · 4

4 x 150–200g tuna steaks
1 Tbsp sesame oil
3 Tbsp white sesame seeds
3 Tbsp black sesame seeds
1 Tbsp canola oil

SAUCE
2 Tbsp smooth peanut butter
2 Tbsp lime juice
1 Tbsp soy sauce
2 tsp honey
a pinch of cayenne pepper
1 tsp sesame oil

1. Rub the tuna all over with the sesame oil. Put half the black and white sesame seeds on a plate and dab 2 of the tuna steaks in the seeds, to coat all over. Repeat with the remaining seeds and steaks.
2. Heat the canola oil in a large frying pan over a medium to high heat. Sear the tuna for 2 minutes per side, to brown the outside and leave the middle pink. Remove, cover loosely with foil and set aside to rest for 2–3 minutes.
3. To make the sauce, mix all the ingredients until well combined.
4. Serve the tuna with the sauce on the side and rice or noodles. Garnish as desired.

125

SPICY SINGAPORE NOODLES

15 m

noodles + 10 m

4

200–250g egg noodles

2 tsp sesame oil

2 Tbsp canola or peanut oil

1 clove garlic, peeled and finely chopped

1 small onion, peeled and finely chopped

½–1 small red chilli, deseeded and finely chopped

2–3 tsp mild curry paste

3 spring onions, trimmed and sliced

a handful of mangetout

12 baby corn, halved lengthways

2 Tbsp soy sauce

350g cooked, peeled and deveined prawns

1. Boil the egg noodles according to packaging instructions, drain most of the water, reserving ½ cup for later use. Put the noodles in a bowl and toss with the sesame oil. Set aside.
2. Heat the canola or peanut oil in a wok over a medium heat. Add the garlic, onion and chilli, and stir-fry for 3 minutes until soft. Stir in the curry paste and cook for 1 minute. Add the vegetables and stir-fry for no more than 2 minutes, to remain crisp. Mix in the soy sauce, the reserved noodle water, noodles and prawns, stir-fry for a further 2–3 minutes to heat through, then serve immediately.

THAI PRAWNS
in TOMATO COCONUT SAUCE

 10 m 10 m 4

2 Tbsp oil

1 large clove garlic, peeled and finely chopped

2cm piece fresh ginger, peeled and finely chopped

500–600g peeled and deveined prawns, thawed if frozen

1 x 400ml can coconut cream

1 stalk lemongrass, twisted and broken in half

2 spring onions, trimmed and finely sliced

½–1 red chilli, deseeded and finely chopped

1 Tbsp tomato paste

1½ Tbsp fish sauce

1 Tbsp fresh lime juice

a handful of fresh coriander and edible flowers for garnishing

1. Heat the oil in a large saucepan over a medium heat and stir-fry the garlic, ginger and prawns for 2 minutes. Add the coconut cream, lemongrass, spring onions, chilli and tomato paste. Bring to the boil and simmer over low heat for 3 minutes. Remove from the heat and stir in the fish sauce and lime juice.

2. Serve with rice or noodles, and coriander and flowers scattered over.

BAKED PRAWN AND CHORIZO RISOTTO

10 m   30 m   4–6

1 Tbsp oil

15g butter plus 20g extra

140g spicy chorizo, skinned and thinly sliced

1 small red onion, peeled and finely chopped

1 clove garlic, peeled and finely chopped

½ tsp dried origanum

1½ cups uncooked Arborio or risotto rice

½ cup dry white wine

4½ cups hot chicken or vegetable stock

300g peeled and deveined prawns, thawed if frozen

12 baby tomatoes, halved

1 Tbsp lemon juice

6 lemon wedges

1. Preheat the oven to 200°C.
2. Heat the oil in a large, ovenproof pan over medium heat on the stove top. Add the 15g butter and as soon as it has melted, gently fry the chorizo, onion and garlic for 4 minutes, until the chorizo has released its red oil and fragrance. Stir the origanum and rice into the buttery oil for 1 minute. Pour in the wine and let it bubble for 2 minutes, until absorbed. Stir in the hot stock and bring to the boil. Transfer the pan to the oven and bake, uncovered, for 16–18 minutes until the liquid is almost absorbed.
3. Remove from the oven and stir well. Check the seasoning, then add the extra butter, prawns and tomatoes. Cover and return to the oven for 5–6 minutes. Remove, stir a little, sprinkle over the lemon juice and serve immediately with lemon wedges.

SIDE
DISHES

POTATO RÖSTIS

15 m   30 m   8–12

These crispy individual servings are perfect as a side dish to a main course, or could be used as a snack or starter, topped with crème fraîche, fresh dill and smoked trout.

2 large potatoes, peeled
½ small onion, peeled
70g butter, melted

1. Preheat the oven to 180°C. Line 2 baking trays with baking paper.

2. Grate the potatoes and onion coarsely into a bowl and mix together. Taking a handful at a time, squeeze all the liquid out (use a cloth if possible), then mix in the butter and season to taste. Pat into flat, round patties, spread evenly about 1cm thick (or use a circle cutter to shape the patties), on the prepared baking trays. The rounds can be any size, to suit the occasion, from little bite-size rounds for finger food parties, about 7cm across, to slightly larger individual portions for a side dish, 8–9cm across. Bake for 25–30 minutes, turning once, until golden and crispy.

3. These are best eaten straightaway, whilst hot and crispy. If they need to be made a day in advance, they can be reheated at the last minute in a hot oven, for 5 minutes, until crispy again, without burning.

CRISPY POTATOES
and PARSNIPS

10 m   1 h   4

½ cup oil
4 medium to large potatoes, peeled
4 large parsnips, peeled

1. Preheat the oven to 180°C. Pour the oil into a large, shallow baking tray.
2. Cut the potatoes lengthways into 2 or 3 pieces. Boil in water for 12 minutes, then drain, cut into chunky cubes and place in the baking tray. Turn to coat in the oil, season and place in the hot oven.
3. Meanwhile, cut the parsnips into quarters lengthways and season.
4. After 30 minutes, remove the baking tray from the oven, turn the potatoes and add the parsnips. Return to the oven, and bake for another 20 minutes, turning the parsnips after 10 minutes, to brown evenly. Drain on kitchen paper and serve hot.

POTATO AND LEEK BAKE

20 m   100 m   4–6

4 large leeks, trimmed and sliced
15g butter
4 medium to large potatoes, peeled, rinsed and thinly sliced

2 cups cream
¾ cup grated cheese of your choice

1. Preheat the oven to 180°C.
2. Wash the leeks well and drain. Melt the butter in a saucepan over a low heat and stir in the leeks. Cover and sweat for 10 minutes until soft, stirring occasionally.
3. Arrange half the potatoes, in an overlapping layer, in a large, shallow baking dish. Pour over 1 cup cream to cover, and season with salt and pepper. Spread the cooked leeks over the potato layer. Repeat with the remaining potato slices and cream, then season again. Top with the grated cheese and cover with a lid or foil. If the dish is very full, place a rimmed baking tray underneath to catch any spills. Bake for 1 hour.
4. Remove the lid or foil and bake for a further 30 minutes, to brown on top.

FLAT BREADS

20 m   12 m   12

These are remarkably easy to make, and a good substitute for tortillas. Delicious with dips.

¾ cup plain yoghurt
1 packed cup* self-raising flour, plus extra for kneading and rolling

1. Mix the yoghurt and flour in a bowl until well combined, then shape into a ball. Sprinkle about 1 Tbsp flour on a wooden board and knead the dough, squashing and turning while incorporating the extra flour. Sprinkle more flour, if necessary, and knead for 5 minutes, until the dough is springy and elastic, but not sticky. Flatten slightly, then cut into quarters. Cut each piece into 3 equal pieces and roll into little golf ball sizes.
2. Sprinkle a little more flour onto the board and roll out each ball into a flat 'pancake' the size of a saucer (13–14cm diameter), turning and flipping over to prevent sticking. Sprinkle more flour when needed.
3. Heat a large, dry frying pan over a medium heat and fry 2 breads at a time, until bubbling and golden-spotted, about 1 minute per side. Transfer to a serving plate, and cover with a tea towel to keep warm, if eating straight away.

*Put the cup into the flour bag and scoop out a compressed cup of flour.

MELBA TOAST

10 m   5 m   4–6

½ loaf slightly stale unsliced white bread or 4 Italian paninis

1. Preheat the grill. Slice the bread, or cut the paninis lengthways, as thinly as possible. Arrange in a single layer on a grill rack in a grill pan. Place under a hot grill for 2–2½ minutes per side, turning when golden. Watch carefully that the toast doesn't burn. Stack upright in a toast rack to keep crisp.

COUSCOUS SALAD
with POMEGRANATE SEEDS

 20 m 10 m 4

1 cup uncooked couscous
1 Tbsp oil
¼ cup pumpkin seeds
½ cup pomegranate seeds
½ cup diced cucumber
½ cup diced feta
3 spring onions, trimmed and sliced
2 sprigs of fresh mint, stalks removed, and larger
leaves torn in half

DRESSING
1 Tbsp lemon juice
1 Tbsp oil

1. Place the couscous in a medium-sized bowl and pour over ¾ cup boiling water. Cover with clingfilm and leave to stand for 10 minutes, until all the water has been absorbed. Fluff up the couscous with a fork and mix in the oil.

2. Meanwhile, heat a small, dry frying pan over a medium heat and toast the pumpkin seeds for 3 minutes, shaking the pan to toast evenly. Transfer to a plate and set aside.

3. Make the dressing by mixing together the lemon juice and oil.

4. To assemble the salad, spoon the couscous onto a large serving platter. Scatter over the pomegranate seeds, cucumber, feta and spring onions. Pour the dressing over the salad, fork through, then scatter over the toasted pumpkin seeds and mint.

135

MIXED TOMATO SALAD
with BASIL and ANCHOVY DRESSING

 20 m   6 m   4–6

2 Tbsp oil
1 large clove garlic, peeled and finely chopped
2 slices ciabatta, torn into bite-size pieces
4 salad tomatoes
150g baby cherry tomatoes
150g baby rosa tomatoes, halved lengthways
a small handful of fresh basil leaves, torn

DRESSING
1 small red onion, peeled and finely chopped
2 anchovies, finely chopped
2 Tbsp red wine vinegar
3 Tbsp olive oil

1. Heat the oil in a frying pan over a low heat and fry half the garlic for 1 minute. Add the ciabatta and toast in the garlic until browned (about 5 minutes). Remove and set aside.
2. Mix the remaining garlic with the dressing ingredients in a salad bowl. Chop the salad tomatoes into bite-size chunks and tip with the juices into the salad bowl. Add the cherry and rosa tomatoes as well as the basil, then toss to coat in the dressing.
3. When ready to serve, scatter over the ciabatta croutons.

RED COLESLAW SALAD

 20 m 3 m 8

2 Tbsp sunflower seeds
1 baby red cabbage, finely sliced
1 baby white cabbage, finely sliced
3 sticks celery, rinsed and sliced
1 small red onion, peeled and thinly sliced
2 large carrots, peeled and grated

DRESSING
¾ cup mayonnaise
¼ cup plain yoghurt
1½ Tbsp cider vinegar
1½ tsp honey

1. Dry-fry the sunflower seeds in a frying pan for
   2–3 minutes, shaking the pan to toast evenly.
   Remove and set aside.
2. Mix the cabbages, celery, onion and carrots in
   a large bowl. Mix the dressing ingredients
   together and toss into the salad.
3. Transfer to a serving dish and
   scatter the sunflower seeds over.

BROCCOLI SALAD
with CRISPY BACON

15 m   10 m   4–6

This can be made a few hours in advance, reserving the dressing until ready to serve. Once the salad is dressed, it is best eaten on the same day.

400g fresh broccoli florets, cut into chunky bite-size pieces
2 Tbsp sunflower seeds
1 Tbsp oil
6 rashers streaky bacon, diced
1 shallot or small red onion, peeled and finely chopped
¼ cup chopped sun-dried tomatoes

DRESSING
½ cup good quality mayonnaise
1 Tbsp white wine vinegar
1 tsp honey

1. Cook the broccoli in boiling salted water over a medium to high heat for 2 minutes, then drain in a sieve and pour cold water over the florets to cool immediately. Leave in the sieve to drain well.
2. Toast the sunflower seeds in a frying pan over a medium heat for 2–3 minutes, shaking the pan to toast evenly. Remove the seeds from the pan and set aside.
3. Heat the oil in the same frying pan over a medium to high heat and fry the bacon for 4 minutes, until crispy. Transfer to a plate lined with kitchen paper, and set aside.
4. Whisk the dressing ingredients together.
5. Assemble the salad by mixing the broccoli, onion and sun-dried tomatoes in a large bowl. Toss in the dressing. When ready to serve, mix in most of the bacon and sunflower seeds, and scatter the rest on top.

NOTE: Salads may be dressed up in many ways, with so many interesting and colourful sprouting beans or seeds, herbs or flowers available. You could also vary the presentation of a single vegetable, such as sugar snap peas, with some shelled and others cut in half lengthways, while spring onions can be cut into thin shreds from both ends, leaving the middle intact, then plunged into cold water until the shreds curl.

BRINJAL, HUMMUS and
SPICY CHICKPEA SALAD

30 m   30 m   4–6

The spicy chickpeas add crunch to this delicious salad, and make a tasty snack at any time. They can be made in advance and stored in a jar for up to a week.

2 medium brinjals, rinsed and sliced lengthways
3 Tbsp oil
½ tsp salt
½ tsp ground cumin
¼ tsp red chilli powder
1 x 400g can chickpeas, drained and rinsed
1 cucumber
250g baby tomatoes
100g sugar snap peas

1 small red onion, peeled and finely sliced
½ cup Hummus (page 27)
a handful of fresh coriander

DRESSING
2 Tbsp oil
1 Tbsp lemon juice
½ tsp ground cumin
1 small clove garlic, peeled and grated

1. Preheat the oven to 180°C.
2. Brush the brinjals on both sides with 2 Tbsp of the oil. Arrange in a single layer on a large baking tray.
3. Mix the remaining oil, salt, cumin and chilli powder in a bowl. Dry the chickpeas on kitchen paper, and toss in the spice mixture. Place in a single layer on a separate baking tray.
4. Roast the brinjals in the top of the oven and the chickpeas in the middle, both for 30 minutes, turning the brinjals once after 15 minutes, and shaking the chickpeas in their tray to turn them over. Remove the brinjals and set aside. Switch the oven off, and leave the chickpeas to cool and dry out in the oven.
5. Slice the cucumber lengthways into ribbons with a vegetable peeler, turning to slice around the core of seeds. Discard the seeds and the first layer of skin on each turn. Arrange the cucumber ribbons on a serving platter. Cut some of the tomatoes and sugar snap peas in half lengthways, then scatter all the tomatoes, peas and onion over the cucumber. Spread a little hummus on each brinjal slice, and dot them in the salad.
6. Whisk the dressing ingredients together, and when ready to serve, drizzle over the salad. Sprinkle the crispy chickpeas over, and top with a few coriander leaves.
7. If you would like a variation to this recipe, add fingers of dry-fried haloumi to the salad just before serving.

GREEN BEANS
with MARINATED MUSHROOMS

20 m   4 m   over-night   6

The mushrooms are best marinated overnight to soak up the flavours, and can also be used as part of an antipasto platter (page 33).

250g small button mushrooms, wiped
250g fine green beans, rinsed, topped and tailed

MARINADE
3 Tbsp white wine vinegar
1 large clove garlic, peeled and finely chopped
½ small red onion, peeled and finely chopped
4 Tbsp oil
2 sprigs of fresh thyme or 1 tsp dried thyme

1. Bring a medium saucepan of salted water to the boil and cook the mushrooms for 2 minutes. Drain and rinse in a sieve in cold water, then drain well.
2. To prepare the marinade, combine the vinegar, garlic, onion, oil and thyme in a glass or ceramic bowl. Stir in the drained mushrooms, ensuring that they're well covered. Marinate overnight.
3. Bring a medium saucepan with a little salted water to the boil and cook the beans for 3–4 minutes, until just al dente. Drain and rinse in a sieve in cold water, then drain well.
4. Assemble the salad by placing the beans on a serving platter, scattering the marinated mushrooms over and pouring some of the marinade over, to dress the salad.

CAULIFLOWER PURÉE

10 m   30 m   4

500g cauliflower florets   ¼ cup milk
30g butter   ¼ cup cream

1. Bring ¾ cup water to the boil in a large saucepan. Add the cauliflower, cover and simmer over low heat for 25 minutes, until soft. Check the water level occasionally. Stir in the butter, milk and cream.
2. Mash or blitz in a blender until the texture is to your liking. Season to taste and gently reheat before serving.
3. A decorative way to serve this side dish is to steam 4 outer baby cabbage leaves for 2–3 minutes to soften them slightly. Separate the leaves into 'cups' and fill them with the purée.

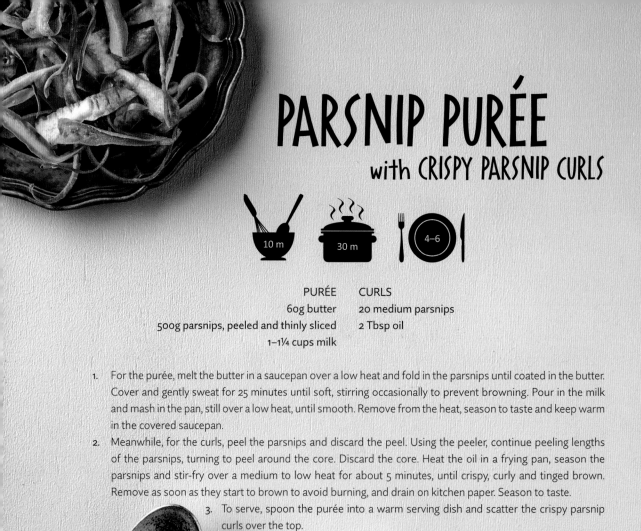

PARSNIP PURÉE
with CRISPY PARSNIP CURLS

10 m   30 m   4–6

PURÉE	CURLS
60g butter	20 medium parsnips
500g parsnips, peeled and thinly sliced	2 Tbsp oil
1–1¼ cups milk	

1. For the purée, melt the butter in a saucepan over a low heat and fold in the parsnips until coated in the butter. Cover and gently sweat for 25 minutes until soft, stirring occasionally to prevent browning. Pour in the milk and mash in the pan, still over a low heat, until smooth. Remove from the heat, season to taste and keep warm in the covered saucepan.
2. Meanwhile, for the curls, peel the parsnips and discard the peel. Using the peeler, continue peeling lengths of the parsnips, turning to peel around the core. Discard the core. Heat the oil in a frying pan, season the parsnips and stir-fry over a medium to low heat for about 5 minutes, until crispy, curly and tinged brown. Remove as soon as they start to brown to avoid burning, and drain on kitchen paper. Season to taste.
3. To serve, spoon the purée into a warm serving dish and scatter the crispy parsnip curls over the top.

KALE CHIPS

 5 m 5–6 m 4

Because these are so light, crispy and delicious, they disappear very quickly, so it's best to make more than you'd normally consider enough!

120g kale
2 Tbsp oil

1. Preheat the oven to 180°C. Line a baking tray with baking paper.
2. Wash the kale and pat dry with kitchen paper. Run a knife down the main stalks to cut off the leaves. Place the leaves on the baking tray in a single layer, and drizzle with the oil. Season and bake for 5–6 minutes until crispy, but not browned.

BUTTERNUT
with SESAME SEEDS

 10 m 40 m 4

1 Tbsp cooking oil
500g butternut, peeled and chopped into cubes
2 tsp sesame oil
2 tsp sesame seeds

1. Preheat the oven to 180°C. Drizzle the cooking oil in a baking tray.
2. Arrange the butternut in the tray, turning the cubes to coat roughly in the oil. Season with salt, and sprinkle over the sesame oil and seeds. Bake for 40 minutes, turning once halfway through. The butternut should be tender and lightly browned.

COURGETTI
with AVOCADO AND PECAN PESTO

 10 m 10 m 4

Spiralised baby marrows make an interesting side dish or a starch-free substitute for spaghetti.

15g butter
400g spiralised baby marrows
12 baby tomatoes
¼ cup crumbled feta

PESTO
½ cup roughly broken pecan nuts
1 ripe avocado, peeled and pip removed
1 Tbsp lemon juice
1 clove garlic, peeled and roughly chopped
25g fresh basil, rinsed and large stalks removed
2 Tbsp oil

1. First make the pesto. Heat a dry frying pan over medium heat and fry the pecan nuts for 2–3 minutes, shaking the pan to roast evenly. Remove and set aside to cool.
2. Make the pesto by blitzing half the nuts with the avocado, lemon juice, garlic, basil and oil in a blender. Season to taste.
3. Heat the butter in a frying pan over a low heat, add the baby marrows, turning to coat with the butter and stir-fry for 2 minutes. Stir in 6 Tbsp pesto (the remaining pesto can be kept in a jar in the fridge for up to a week) and top with the tomatoes. Cover and heat through over medium heat for 4 minutes, turning occasionally, until the baby marrows are tender but still firm.
4. Serve hot, sprinkled with the remaining nuts and the feta.

ROASTED
VINE TOMATOES
with PESTO

 2 m 12–15 m 4

This simple and refreshing side dish is excellent with lamb, barbecued meat or grilled fish.

2 Tbsp oil
16–20 vine tomatoes
1 Tbsp basil pesto

1. Preheat the oven to 180°C. Drizzle half the oil in a shallow roasting tin.
2. Place the tomatoes, still on the vine, in the roasting tin. Mix the pesto with the remaining oil and drizzle over the tomatoes. Roast for 12–15 minutes, until softened. Serve on the side.

STUFFED BRINJALS

15 m   25 m   4

2 large brinjals
1 Tbsp oil
1 medium onion, peeled and finely chopped
80g button mushrooms, wiped and finely chopped

1 small clove garlic, peeled and finely chopped
1 large tomato, skinned and chopped
½ cup grated cheese of your choice

1. Set the oven grill on high.
2. Cook the brinjals in a large pan of boiling water for 10 minutes until softened. Remove and allow to cool for a few minutes, then slice in half, lengthways, and cut or scoop out the middle, leaving about 1cm of flesh inside the skin. Try not to cut through the skin, as this will be your 'bowl'. Roughly chop the scooped out brinjal flesh and set aside.
3. Heat the oil in a frying pan over a medium heat, and gently fry the onion for 4 minutes. Add the mushrooms, garlic, tomato, salt and pepper, and stir-fry for a further 3–4 minutes. Mix in the chopped brinjal, and generously heap the mixture into the brinjal skins. Sprinkle the grated cheese over and grill for 3–4 minutes under the hot grill, until bubbling and golden.
4. Serve immediately.

DESSERTS

LEMON and GRANADILLA
CHEESECAKE

20 m 7 m over-night 6–8

This no-bake cheesecake is particularly colourful and flavoursome with the inclusion of fresh granadillas. When the fruits are not in season, you could use canned granadilla pulp but, because it is much sweeter, use half the quantity of icing sugar in the filling.

BASE
200g ginger biscuits, crushed
80g butter, melted

FILLING
1x 250g block full-fat cream cheese
1 x 250g tub mascarpone
1 cup whipping cream
4 Tbsp lemon juice (from ±1 lemon)
4 Tbsp icing sugar
pulp of 4 ripe granadillas or 1 x 110g can granadilla pulp

TOPPING
pulp of 4 ripe granadillas
4 tsp sugar
2 Tbsp water
1 tsp lemon juice
Alternatively use 1 x 110g can granadilla pulp (omit the sugar, water and lemon juice)

1. Lightly spray a 20cm springform baking tin with oil. Line the base with baking paper.
2. Mix the crushed biscuits with the melted butter and press into the base of the prepared tin. Chill in the fridge until needed.
3. For the filling, place the cream cheese, mascarpone, cream, lemon juice and icing sugar in a large mixing bowl and slowly beat until smooth and thickening (about 2 minutes on low speed with an electric beater). Do not overbeat as the mixture will become grainy*. Stir in the granadilla pulp then spread the mixture over the biscuit base and chill while making the topping.
4. To make the topping, heat the fresh granadilla pulp, sugar, water and lemon juice in a small saucepan. Simmer for 5 minutes and strain into a bowl, squashing the pulp through the sieve with a spoon. Add about ¾ tsp seeds back into the pulp. Leave to cool then pour over the cheesecake. If using the canned pulp, simply pour it over the cheesecake. In either case, chill overnight to set.

*If the mixture starts to become grainy, gently hand-whisk an extra few tablespoons of fresh cream into the mixture, to rescue the texture.

LEMON MERINGUE NESTS

30 m   1½ h   2 h   16–24 nests   330 ml curd

½ cup whipped cream for topping
fresh berries and/or figs for topping

MERINGUE
2 egg whites, room temperature
½ tsp lemon juice
½ cup castor sugar

LEMON CURD
2 large lemons
½ cup sugar
60g butter
2 eggs, lightly whisked

1. Preheat the oven to 90°C. Line 2 baking sheets with baking paper.
2. To make the meringue, beat the egg whites with the lemon juice until soft peaks form (do not overbeat). Gradually add the castor sugar, one spoonful at a time, beating after each addition. The glossy mixture should hold its shape. Spoon into a piping bag fitted with a star nozzle, or plastic food bag and snip the corner. Pipe the mixture onto the baking sheets, in 4–5cm circles, forming a spiral base. Pipe a second ring around the edge, to create a little nest. Ensure that there is a small space between each nest. Bake on the lower shelf of the oven for 1½ hours, then switch off the heat, leaving the meringues to cool and dry out in the oven for about 2 hours.
3. These can be made well in advance and kept for a long time in a sealed container.
4. For the lemon curd, finely grate the lemon rind (avoiding the bitter, white pith) into a saucepan. Cut the lemons in half and squeeze out the juice into the same pan. Add the sugar, butter and eggs. Heat gently over a medium to low heat, whisking constantly until just thickened, to prevent the eggs from scrambling. Strain into a bowl and leave to cool. Chill until needed. The mixture will thicken further in the fridge.
5. When ready to serve, whip the cream until soft peaks form then swirl in the lemon curd. Spoon the mixture into the meringue nests and top with a few fresh berries and halved figs.
6. Any unused lemon curd can be kept in a sealed jar in the fridge for up to 2 weeks.

AMARULA SABAYON
with BERRIES and BISCOTTI

6 m   10 m   4

'Sabayon' if you're French, or 'zabaglione' if you're Italian, this is traditionally a luxurious rich, foamy custard, flavoured with sweet Marsala wine and made at the last minute before serving. In order to bring this delicious dessert to your table without the last-minute frenzy, this version may be made in advance. It is rich and creamy, and as a variation it uses Amarula, but you may use any sweet flavouring of your choice.

2 cups fresh berries (your choice)
biscotti biscuits, crushed

SABAYON
4 egg yolks
4 Tbsp sugar
4 Tbsp Amarula cream liqueur

1. To make the sabayon, hand-whisk the egg yolks and sugar in a heatproof bowl over simmering water, for 2 minutes until foamy. Add the Amarula, whisking constantly until the mixture is a pale caramel colour with a thick and creamy texture (7–8 minutes). Remove from the heat and set the bowl in a shallow container of cold water to chill quickly, before the eggs begin to scramble. Stir occasionally while cooling, then refrigerate until needed.

2. To serve, place ½ cup fresh berries in the bottom of individual glasses, spoon some sabayon over and top with a little crushed biscotti.

There are boundless variations to this dessert, depending on your creative choice of flavouring and how you wish to serve it. A few ideas are:

• Use 2 Tbsp Kahlúa instead of Amarula in the sabayon and pour over coffee granita, made with 1 cup of strong coffee mixed with 2 tsp sugar, then frozen and occasionally agitated to break down the crystals. Defrost a little, before forking through and serving in individual glasses with the sabayon spooned over.

• To make a luxurious custard, when the sabayon is completely cool, whip ½ cup cream to soft peak stage and fold into the egg mixture. Chill, then spoon over a platter of fresh fruits.

• Alternatively, fold in the cream and freeze. Serve as a semifreddo with raspberries or strawberries.

MANGO CREAM

10 m   4–6

This is a beautiful and colourful
dessert that is also delicious, easy
and very quick to make. There
are many juicy varieties of mango
on the market, but avoid
the fibrous, stringy sort,
such as Tommy Atkins.

2 large ripe mangoes
2 Tbsp freshly squeezed lemon juice
(or more, to taste, if the mangoes are
very sweet)
2 tsp icing sugar, or to taste
1 cup thick cream
fresh raspberries for topping
wafer cigars for serving (optional)

1. Peel and cut the mangoes around the
   pip, reserving half a mango for the
   topping. Chop and put the rest of the
   mangoes in a blender with the lemon
   juice and blitz until smooth. Blend in
   the sugar, as desired. Add the cream
   and blend for 1 minute, then pour into
   a serving dish or individual glasses.
2. Dice the reserved mango and arrange
   on the mango cream. Top with a few
   raspberries and chill until ready to
   serve. Serve with wafer cigars, if using.

CRÈME BRÛLÉE

This classic favourite needs to be prepared in advance to set to a thick, creamy consistency. It can be made with whipping cream, although double cream will give a richer finish. Ideally, use shallow, wide dishes to get the full benefit of the brûlée (burnt) sugar on top.

2 cups cream
1 vanilla pod or 1 tsp vanilla extract
2 Tbsp castor sugar
4 egg yolks, lightly beaten
8 tsp demerara sugar for serving

1. Preheat the oven to 140°C. Place 4 x 150ml ramekins in a deep baking tin.
2. Pour the cream into a heatproof bowl with the vanilla pod or extract. Set the bowl over a small saucepan of simmering water and gently heat the cream until almost boiling, with bubbles around the edge. Remove from the heat and take out the vanilla pod (but keep for future use*). Stir in the castor sugar to dissolve, then lightly whisk in the beaten egg yolks.
3. Pour the mixture into the 4 ramekins, and carefully pour enough hot water into the baking tin to reach halfway up the sides of the ramekins. Avoid splashing any water into the ramekins. Bake for 45 minutes, until the sides are just set and the centres still wobbly. Remove the ramekins from the hot water and allow to cool completely before covering them with clingfilm and chilling to firm up in the fridge overnight.
4. At least 1 hour before serving, sprinkle 2 teaspoons of demerara sugar evenly over each ramekin, then glaze with a blowtorch, or place under a very hot grill for 3–5 minutes, until the sugar melts. This will set to a crisp, caramelised crust. Set aside, or chill until 30 minutes before serving. Serve at room temperature.

*Use the seeds for flavouring cakes, etc, and the used pod may be stored in a bag of castor sugar to flavour the sugar.

CHOCOLATE CRÉMEUX CUPS
with STRAWBERRY DIPPERS

This is an easy, 10-minute dessert that is best made the day before serving.
As it is very rich, a little goes a long way.

160g plain dark chocolate (70% cocoa), broken into small pieces
2 egg yolks
½ cup thick cream
½ cup full-cream milk
½ tsp vanilla essence
18 medium strawberries, rinsed and hulled
6 long wooden toothpicks or skewers
6 cigar wafers (optional)

1. Put the chocolate into a heatproof mixing bowl or glass measuring jug. Place a sieve over the bowl.
2. Lightly beat the egg yolks in a separate heatproof bowl.
3. Heat the cream and milk in a small saucepan over a medium heat for 2–3 minutes, until almost boiling, with bubbles around the edge. Pour onto the egg yolks and whisk continually, to combine. Strain the mixture into the chocolate bowl, covering all the chocolate pieces, and leave for 1 minute to melt. Add the vanilla and whisk until smooth. Pour into individual small pots or glasses and allow to cool. Chill for at least 4 hours or overnight.
4. When ready to serve, thread 3 strawberries onto each wooden skewer, and place in each chocolate pot. Add a cigar wafer, if using, and a teaspoon to serve.
5. This recipe may be varied with the addition of a little alcohol instead of the vanilla, and other fruits, or decorations on top. Try:
   - Frangelico with toasted hazelnuts on top.
   - Grand Marnier with orange segments on top.
   - Strawberries with crushed meringues sprinkled over.

FLOURLESS
CHOCOLATE TORTE

20 m · 35–40 m · 8

Both decadent and wheat-free, this dessert may be served in two different ways. Initially it is light and airy, and if served within a few hours, can be filled with whipped cream swirled with a chocolate ganache. If served the next day, when it is more fudgy in the middle, fill it with whipped cream and fresh strawberries. Either way, fill at the last minute. This type of torte naturally subsides in the centre and has a raised outer edge.

250g plain dark chocolate (70% cocoa), broken into small squares
125g butter, cubed
4 eggs
a pinch of salt
¼ cup castor sugar
1 tsp vanilla essence

GANACHE AND CREAM TOPPING
¼ cup whipping cream
90g chocolate
¼ cup extra cream

STRAWBERRIES AND CREAM TOPPING
¼ cup whipping cream
400g strawberries, rinsed and hulled

1. Preheat the oven to 180°C. Lightly grease a 22cm springform tin and line the base with baking paper.
2. Put the chocolate pieces in a heatproof bowl with the butter cubes. Either melt in the microwave for 1 minute or melt over a small saucepan of simmering water, and stir until smooth. Remove from the heat and cool.
3. Separate the whites of 2 eggs into a mixing bowl, and put the yolks into another large mixing bowl. Whisk the whites with the salt until soft peaks form (about 2 minutes). Using the same whisk, beat the yolks with the remaining 2 whole eggs, castor sugar and vanilla essence until pale, thick and creamy (about 3 minutes). Gently fold in the cooled chocolate. Mix a spoonful of the egg whites into the chocolate mixture. Carefully fold in the remaining whites, keeping the mixture light.
4. Pour into the prepared springform tin and bake for 35–40 minutes, until set and a slight crust has formed on top. Leave to cool in the tin on a cooling rack. Turn out of the tin onto a dish just before serving.
5. **If using Ganache and Cream Topping:** When ready to serve, whip the cream until soft and fluffy. Melt the chocolate in the extra cream and stir until smooth. When cool, swirl the mixture into the whipped cream, and fill the torte.
6. **If using Strawberries and Cream Topping:** When ready to serve, whip the cream until soft and fluffy. Cut any large strawberries in half. Fill the torte with the cream and arrange the strawberries on top.

SPICED SEMIFREDDO
with POMEGRANATE SEEDS

Made with a rich custard and cream, this dessert requires no churning and is ready to serve straight from the freezer.

1 egg
4 egg yolks
6 Tbsp honey
1 tsp ground cinnamon
¼ tsp ground nutmeg
1¼ cups whipping cream
½ cup pomegranate seeds

1. Line a 1-litre loaf tin with clingfilm, allowing the clingfilm to extend over the edge.
2. Fill a small saucepan quarter full with water and bring to the boil. Turn down the heat and allow the water to simmer slowly. Beat the egg, yolks and honey in a heatproof bowl over the simmering water with either a balloon whisk or with an electric, hand-held whisk at low speed for 7 minutes until pale, creamy and frothy. Remove from the heat, add the cinnamon and nutmeg and continue whisking to cool and thicken, for a further 8 minutes.
3. Whip the cream separately until soft peaks form (about 4 minutes). Pour the egg mixture with the cinnamon and nutmeg into the cream and whisk for 30 seconds to combine. Pour into the prepared loaf tin, and cover over completely with clingfilm. Freeze for at least 6 hours or overnight.
4. To serve, turn out of the tin onto a platter and scatter with the pomegranate seeds. Serve immediately, as it doesn't take long for the semifreddo to melt.

CHAMPAGNE SORBET

 5 m 5 m 12 h

 500 ml 4–6

This recipe works well with Champagne or any dry sparkling wine. Keep any unused sorbet in the freezer for up to 2 weeks.

½ cup sugar*
½ cup water*
1¼ cups dry sparkling wine
fresh strawberries for serving
fresh mint for serving

1. To make the simple sugar syrup, combine the sugar and water in a saucepan and bring to the boil. Simmer over a low heat for 2 minutes, stirring occasionally, to dissolve the sugar. Remove from the heat and pour into a heatproof bowl to cool.

2. Stir in the sparkling wine, then transfer to a plastic container with a lid, and freeze. After 6 hours or longer, whisk or blitz in a blender until smooth, to prevent any crystals from forming. Freeze for a minimum of another 6 hours, or overnight, until needed.

3. When ready to serve, put a few halved strawberries in glass tumblers, and top with 1 or 2 scoops of sorbet and a mint leaf. Serve immediately, as the sorbet is soft and melts quickly.

*This ratio is essential for the basic syrup, to ensure the correct texture of the sorbet – too little sugar will make the sorbet too icy, while too much will cause it to be slushy.

LEMON and MINT
GRANITA

 10 m 5 m 12 h 500 ml  10–15

This is zingy and refreshing, served in a small glass (such as a large shot glass) with or without the alcohol. It is ideal for drinks and snacks parties or as a dessert.

½ cup sugar
1 cup water
½ cup lemon juice

¼ cup finely chopped fresh mint, plus extra small leaves for serving
vodka or gin for serving (optional)

1. To make the granita syrup, combine the sugar and water in a saucepan and bring to the boil. Simmer over a low heat for 2 minutes, stirring occasionally, to dissolve the sugar. Remove from the heat and pour into a heatproof bowl to cool. Stir in the lemon juice and mint, then transfer to a wide, shallow plastic container with a lid, and freeze for 12 hours or overnight.

2. Before serving, allow to thaw slightly, then break the iced mixture into small granules with a fork, and spoon into the glasses. Either pour a dash of vodka or gin over, or serve plain, with a small mint leaf in each glass.

VANILLA CHAI TEA
PANNACOTTA

2 m · 15 m · 5 h–overnight · 4–6

For the best result, make this the day before serving.

1 cup double or thick cream
1 cup whipping cream
2 Tbsp sugar
3 vanilla Chai teabags
1½ gelatine leaves
Crystallised Rose Petals for decorating (optional) (page 166)
fresh berries for serving

1. Mix the two creams and the sugar in a saucepan, and bring to the boil over a medium heat, stirring to dissolve the sugar. Remove from the heat and add the teabags. Leave to infuse for 10 minutes.
2. Meanwhile, soak the gelatine leaves in cold water for a minimum of 5 minutes to soften.
3. Remove the teabags and re-heat the cream until bubbles start forming around the edge. Remove from the heat.
4. Squeeze the water from the gelatine, and stir the gelatine into the hot cream, until it dissolves. Pour into 4–6 ramekins or small cups. Allow to cool completely, then cover with clingfilm and chill in the fridge for at least 5 hours, or preferably overnight.
5. When ready to serve, dip the base of each ramekin or cup into hot water for 10 seconds, then turn out into individual serving bowls. Decorate with crystallised rose petals, if using, and serve with fresh berries.

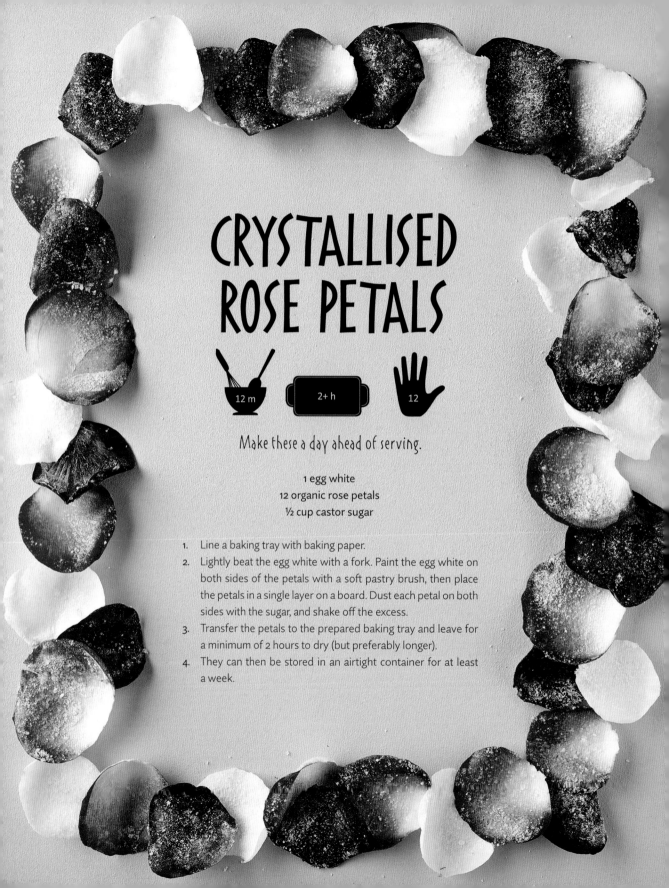

CRYSTALLISED ROSE PETALS

12 m | 2+ h | 12

Make these a day ahead of serving.

1 egg white
12 organic rose petals
½ cup castor sugar

1. Line a baking tray with baking paper.
2. Lightly beat the egg white with a fork. Paint the egg white on both sides of the petals with a soft pastry brush, then place the petals in a single layer on a board. Dust each petal on both sides with the sugar, and shake off the excess.
3. Transfer the petals to the prepared baking tray and leave for a minimum of 2 hours to dry (but preferably longer).
4. They can then be stored in an airtight container for at least a week.

MARSHMALLOW ICING
for CUPCAKES

20 m   24

This is a beautiful icing for vanilla cupcakes, using Swiss meringue
in which the egg white is partially cooked.

4 large egg whites   ¼ tsp cream of tartar
1 cup castor sugar   1 tsp vanilla essence

1. Combine the egg whites, castor sugar and cream of tartar in a large heatproof bowl over a saucepan of simmering water. Ensure that the water does not touch the bowl. Whisk until the sugar is dissolved and the mixture is warm to the touch (3–4 minutes).
2. Remove from the heat and continue to whisk, starting on a low speed and gradually increasing to high, until the glossy mixture forms stiff peaks that hold their shape (5–7 minutes). Fold in the vanilla essence.
3. Spoon the mixture into a piping bag fitted with a large star nozzle, or a plastic food bag and snip the corner. To make a swirl of icing, start piping a ring of icing around the edge of the cupcake, and keep going in an overlapping spiral towards the centre, finishing with a peak in the centre, like a softserve ice cream.

TOASTED
MACADAMIA NUT BLONDIES

20 m 23 m 1 h 16

Fudgy and addictive, these white-chocolate versions of brownies are perfect for bite-size, any-time treats.

½ cup macadamia nuts
180g white chocolate, broken into small pieces, plus 50g for topping
70g butter, cubed
2 eggs
½ cup castor sugar
1 tsp vanilla essence
¾ cup cake flour
½ tsp baking powder
a pinch of salt

1. Preheat the oven to 180°C. Lightly spray a 20cm-square baking tin with a little oil and line the base with baking paper.
2. Roughly chop the nuts into pea-size chunks. Heat a dry frying pan over medium heat and fry the nuts for 3 minutes, shaking the pan to toast evenly. Transfer them to a cold dish.
3. Put the chocolate and butter into a medium-sized, heatproof bowl. Either melt in the microwave in two 30-second bursts, stirring in between to avoid burning the chocolate, then stirring until smooth, or melt over a small saucepan of simmering water, stirring until smooth and ensuring no water splashes into the mixture. Remove from the heat and allow to cool.
4. In a large mixing bowl, beat the eggs, castor sugar and vanilla essence until pale and creamy (3–4 minutes). Stir in the cooled chocolate. Sift the flour, baking powder and salt into the mixture, add the nuts and fold in gently until well combined, but do not overmix.
5. Pour the mixture into the prepared baking tin, spreading it evenly, and bake in the centre of the oven for 20 minutes. It is ready when the centre is just set and the top and edges slightly golden. Allow to cool for 10 minutes in the tin, then run a knife around the edge and turn over onto a board, to cool the underside. Turn over onto a rack and when completely cool, melt the extra chocolate and drizzle over the top. Leave to set for 1 hour at room temperature, then cut into 16 squares.

RED VELVET CUPCAKES

35 m — 15 m — 12

1¼ cups cake flour	1–2 Tbsp red food colouring
½ tsp baking powder	½ cup buttermilk
1 Tbsp cocoa powder	
a pinch of salt	ICING
60g soft butter	½ x 250g tub cream cheese
¾ cup sugar	1 packed cup icing sugar
½ cup oil	1 tsp lemon juice
2 eggs	fresh raspberries for decorating
1 tsp vanilla essence	

1. Preheat the oven to 180°C. Line a 12-cup muffin tin with cupcake cases.
2. Sift the flour, baking powder, cocoa and salt into a mixing bowl.
3. Beat the butter and sugar together until creamy, then beat in the oil. Beat in the eggs and vanilla essence, followed by the food colouring. Slowly beat in half the flour mixture with half the buttermilk, then add the remaining flour mixture and buttermilk, and beat until just combined.
4. Spoon into the cupcake cases and bake for 15 minutes. They are ready when the top is springy and a toothpick inserted in the centre comes out clean. Allow to cool for 5 minutes in the tin, then transfer to a cooling rack to cool completely.
5. For the icing, beat the cream cheese, icing sugar and lemon juice together until smooth. Spoon the mixture into a piping bag fitted with a star nozzle, or into a plastic bag with the tip of the corner snipped, then pipe in spirals over the cupcakes. Top each cupcake with a fresh raspberry.

 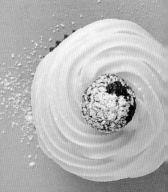

CARROT CAKE

35 m   50–55 m   1 h   12–14

2 cups cake flour
2 tsp baking powder
2 tsp bicarbonate of soda
½ tsp salt
2 tsp ground cinnamon
2 tsp mixed spice
4 eggs
1½ cups soft brown sugar
1¼ cups oil
2 tsp vanilla essence

1 cup pecan nuts
3 cups grated carrots (±375g)*

ICING
200g cream cheese, at room temperature
90g butter, softened
2 cups icing sugar, sifted
2 tsp lemon juice
pecan nuts and/or Crystallised Rose Petals
   (page 166) for decorating

1. Preheat the oven to 170°C. Lightly spray or brush a 24–26cm cake tin (for 1 large single-layer cake) or 2 x 22cm round cake tins (for a smaller, double-layer cake) with a little oil. Line the base of the tin/s with baking paper.
2. Sift the flour, baking powder, bicarbonate of soda, salt, cinnamon and mixed spice into a large mixing bowl.
3. In another bowl, beat the eggs, brown sugar, oil and vanilla essence. Add this mixture to the flour mixture and fold in well.
4. Put the nuts into a plastic bag and break them into small chunks with a rolling pin. Fold the carrots and nuts into the cake batter, then pour the batter into the cake tin/s and bake in the centre of the oven for 45–50 minutes for a large cake or 35–37 minutes for 2 smaller cakes. Test for readiness by inserting a skewer into the centre of each cake; it should come out clean. When done, allow to cool in the tins for 5 minutes, then turn them out onto a rack and allow to cool completely.
5. To make the icing, beat the cream cheese with the butter, then slowly beat in the icing sugar and lemon juice until smooth and creamy. Sandwich the two cooled cakes together with some of the icing and use the rest to ice the top. Alternatively, spread all of it over the top of the larger, cooled cake. Decorate with pecan nuts and/ or crystallised rose petals.

*For a more moist cake texture, use finely grated carrots.

RECIPE INDEX

Page numbers in **bold** indicate photographs.

174

175

INDEX